Boswell's Coast

Patrick Boswell

Dudley Publishing
Norfolk 2010

Boswell's Coast
First Published 2010

Published By Dudley Publishing

Dudley Publishing
1 Milebridge Farm Cottage,
Spinks Lane,
Wymondham,
Norfolk,
NR18 0SR.

British Library Cataloguing in Publication Data
Boswell, Patrick 1942
Boswell's Coast

A CIP catalogue record for this book is available
from the British Library

ISBN: 978-0-9565227-0-2

Design and Layout
Rachael Evitt

PRINTED IN GREAT BRITAIN
by Breckland Print

Front Cover Painting; Cliff Study, West Runton
Back Cover Painting; Cliff Study, East Runton

Boswell's Coast

Patrick Boswell

Contents

This book is dedicated to the
memory of my sister,
Anne Boswell-Sands
a free spirit.

Acknowledgements

I would like to acknowledge and say a big thank you to all those who have helped in the preparation and production of this book. In particular to Rachael Evitt for her never failing enthusiasm in making sense of my somewhat vague instructions of how I wanted the book to appear. Pulling it all together and producing a fine publication. Well done Rachael.

It goes without saying that my wife, Christine, once again sat at her computer for many hours typing my diary entries about the weather, wind speed and direction of the sun. A putty medal goes to her for sheer dogged determination to see the job through.

My daughter Natalie who accompanied me on various painting expeditions, so to my friend and fellow painter Paul Darley for his continuing support and company painting at various locations. Daughter Sophie for her support from The Shears in Wiltshire and son-in law James for his practical support.

Many thanks go to Charlotte Crawley , Director of the East Anglia Art Fund at the Castle Museum, Norwich for writing the foreword.

I am indebted to the following galleries who have hung my work over the years;

Tizzy Fairhurst of Fairhurst Gallery, Norwich; Andrew Wilson of A&K Gallery, Harpenden; Frames Gallery, St. Giles Norwich; The Grapevine Gallery, Norwich; The Assembly Rooms, Norwich; Mandells Gallery, Norwich; Jorn Langberg of Langham Fine Art; Crome gallery, Norwich; Melinda Raker of Croxton Park, Thetford; Shepherds Market Gallery, London; Robert, Daphne and Rachael Dawson-Smith at The Saracen's Head Restaurant at Wolterton; The Garden Gallery, Southwold; Thompson's Gallery, Aldeburgh; Ringstead Gallery, Burnham Market and The Flint Gallery, Blakeney.

The following lists of books have proved invaluable in providing historical and factual details about artists who lived and worked on this fabulous coastline;

Norfolk Coastal Sketches by David Poole, Norfolk Beaches by Steve and Alyson Appleyard, Making Waves (Artists in Southwold) by Ian Collins, A Broad Canvas (Art in East Anglia since 1880) by Ian Collins, Southwold (an earthly paradise) by Geoffrey C. Munn, Wide Skies (a century of painting and painters in Norfolk) by Adrienne May and Brian Watts, Elements of the North Norfolk Coast by David North and Martin Hayward Smith, All Our Yesterdays, Norfolk by Michael Shaw, various books by Edward Seago including A canvas to Cover, Edward Seago by James Reid and Ron Ransom.

Above all it is the people I met on the way that I wish to say my biggest thanks from bird watchers to dog walkers and jolly café owners, all helped unknowingly to complete my task. They provided the enthusiastic support for my work, directed me to the best spots to paint and helped fill my diaries with the minutiae of interesting facts. Thanks a lot.

Last and by no means least, those patrons who have purchased my works over the years, in particular John and Shelia Lawrence, Liz and Bernard Bryan, Mr and Mrs. Telford Shute and many others too numerous to mention.

Introduction

Call me an old romantic but my initial thoughts for my coastal journey would that it be made by horse and trap or simply travelling with a caravan, stopping every night in a new village or coastal field, gazing at the stars or sunset as I reflected on each days adventures. The reality, I am afraid, was much more simple. I travelled frequently to the coast by car, don't ask me how many miles, and slept peacefully in my bed each night.

My journey was partly inspired by the book 'Norfolk Coastal Sketches' by David Poole in which he depicts the coast in a series of pencil drawings from Kings Lynn to Great Yarmouth. I decided to go considerably further by depicting in oil every village and hamlet starting at Aldeburgh in Suffolk and northwards through to Kings Lynn in west Norfolk. I don't think I realized when I set out in August 2008, the extent of my task in having to navigate the little country lanes and then choosing a spot as near or on the coast as possible. I relied considerably on the local people when I was not sure of the area, and bowed to their better judgement at all times. I soon realized if I was just to simply paint on the beach each day, I would have produced a book with a mass of paintings of sea, beach and cliffs, not too exciting. So, I endeavoured where possible, to concentrate on what I do best, with figures and buildings to add to the scene. Quite often the painting dictated itself as I trod the path of famous artists who had made a certain village or beach view their own; Seago, with his coastal paintings of Walcot and Waxham, Campbell Mellon with his lively figurative scenes of Gorleston and Great Yarmouth depicting an era of bathing machines and beach tents. Further north I was reminded of the wonderful paintings by Paul Darley of the fishermen and beach scenes at Cromer which he has made his own; Cox's paintings of the harbour at Wells and Walter Dexter's Kings Lynn. I just hope, in my small way I came close to my elders and betters' achievements.

My painting journeys would start early as I loaded the car with box easel, sundry bags and painting boards of all descriptions. I had to be very organized not to forget that pair of fingerless gloves or woolly hat. Mountains of sandwiches would be made but, I must confess, I visited some lovely cafes and small restaurants along the way. I have sampled prawn baguettes at Aldeburgh, delicious home made soup at Winterton, not to mention whelks and cockles from Wells. I could go on to mention that I have been offered tea and coffee by locals and holidaymakers alike, it's a wonder I ever finished my task.

I think the best part of my trip wqs made more enjoyable along the way by dog walkers and bird watchers who stopped to chat. I was quite surprised that even I became a bit of a twitcher after a while. I thought I knew my coast but every day was quite a new experience, whether it was a jumble of coastal buildings at Scratby or the stunning beach of Holkham Bay. Although my journey is over I feel my life has been enriched and I hope the reader will find a similar experience.

Foreword

Patrick Boswell's career has taken him in several directions over the years, but his heart it seems has always been in pictures. His Victorian forebears were steeped in the artistic life of Norwich as carvers and gilders to Cotman, Stark and various Norwich School painters. Later Boswells became picture dealers as well, acting for Munnings. This long family association has given Patrick a great knowledge of the physical landscape of East Anglia, together with its ever-changing moods and seasonal swings. In Patrick's new book – Boswell's Coast – his great feel for the sea boundaries of Norfolk and Suffolk finds fluent expression in an exhilarating exploration of all sorts of coastal scenes.

In his previous book – Boswell's Norwich, published in 2008, most of the pictures were enlivened by some of Patrick's sketchy figures, plying the city's streets. In addition, we the readers were illuminated, and often amused by diary jottings he made on the day he painted a particular view, and we read his brief weather notes with interest. From Canaletto to Constable and down to the present day, artists have helped their admirers to understand their paintings via similar scribbles and notes observing the date, place, weather etc. The immediacy of Patrick Boswell's colourful oils is one of their many appealing characteristics, although it is a trait we more often associate with watercolours. Patrick paints it like it was – there and then. In Coast, many scenes are well-known favourites – The House in the Clouds at Thorpeness, Walberswick Beach, Gorleston lighthouse and harbour, Cley Mill and Burnham Overy Staithe. Others are just as much a part of that coastal experience, be they Sizewell village, Yarmouth Hippodrome or the Coal Slipway at Mundesley – but they often are ignored by painters seeking more typical picture-postcard subjects. Patrick's compositions are much more

varied and he embraces unspoilt natural features just as enthusiastically as complicated architectural structures like Sandringham House, Paston Great Barn or St. Andrew's Church at Covehithe.

At the end of May last year my extended family went back to the Hampshire coast to celebrate a special birthday. The sun shone and over the weekend we all enjoyed a brilliant family party. That visit however highlighted for us all two important things. Firstly, just how crowded so much of the south coast of England has become, and secondly, how incredibly lucky we are in East Anglia to still be able to feel we have great swathes of the edge of Norfolk and Suffolk to ourselves! In plenty of Patrick's beach pictures - the sea sparkles and the sand is almost white under a brilliant blue sky, but the beach is virtually deserted.

Boswell's Coast reflects that geographic isolation which many of us treasure, and it celebrates why holidays or walks by the sea in Suffolk and Norfolk have such enduring appeal.

Charlotte Crawley
Director of the East Anglia Art Fund

Lighthouse and harbour, Gorleston

Cley

The Artist

From an early age I was conscious that I had an artistic family background in that I learned about artists in my family. Aunt Faith was a portraitist who had paintings hung in the Stock Exchange in London. Aunt Ruth, an antique dealer, had her portrait painted as a young girl by A.J.Munnings. My sister Anne was an antique dealer and had a 'good eye for pictures', as they say. My brother Roger too, was at one time training for architecture but ended up as a bomb disposal expert. The family thought that he would go out with a bang, but thankfully didn't before retirement.

It was further back in time that the family had a long association with the Norwich School of Artists, culminating with one of my forebears being made a Freeman of Norwich, something continued to this day with male members of the family. They were originally carvers and gilders to Norwich artists and eventually would go on to have their own galleries in London Street run by Great Grandfather James and his brother Samuel. The family were the main agents for A.J.Munnings in Norwich.

At the turn of the 20th Century it was Major Bernard Boswell who continued the gallery as Boswell's in Tombland and I myself, latterly, ran Boswell's Fine Art from Orford Yard in Norwich for many years before taking up painting as a full time artistic occupation. I could wax lyrical about artists who influenced me, from Ken Howard to Bernard Dunstan, but I suppose like all things one goes back to early influences. Clara Leeds at Unthank College in Norwich, Mr. Robinson at Langley School and perhaps the biggest influence of them all, Mary Young, a retired lecturer in art from Hornsey College in London who gave me early encouragement from her studio in Southrepps.

Although painting and drawing were important to me all my life, my career path over the years has been diverse if nothing else. Trained originally as a classical French chef at Browns Hotel in London, my career led me to the Hilton Hotel, Royal garden Hotel and eventually to the South of France for further training at The Grand Hotel at Cap Ferrat, to the Hotel Juana, Juan Les Pins and finally to the Croix Blanche at Chamonix. Fluent French has helped me to direct tourists in Norwich on many occasions and in latter years found my way round a decent wine list if nothing else. Garden furniture design

and property renovation too have been occupations that have taken my time over the years but it was always back to the paintings that kept my interest alive and I am sure it will continue to do so for many a year.

My first book was of Norwich where I was born and bred so I had no difficulty in undertaking this coastal journey for a second book for I have lived and worked for many years near our beautiful coastline.

W. BOSWELL,
CARVER, GILDER,
Upholsterer, Cabinet and Chair Maker,
48, LONDON STREET, NORWICH.
Artists' Colourman.
The Best House for FIRST-CLASS FURNITURE,
LOOKING GLASSES, PAPER HANGINGS, &c.
Old Furniture Re-covered, Repaired, or Cleaned.

Boswell's Coast

1. Fresh Fish, Aldeburgh	1.5" x 9"
2. The Moot Hall, Aldeburgh	11" x 9"
3. Flora Tea Rooms, Dunwich Beach	14" x 10"
4. The White Hart, Blythburgh	11.5" x 9"
5. By the Blyth, Walberswick	16" x 11"
6. The Beach, Walberswick	12" x 10"
7. Gun Hill Café, Southwold	16" x 12"
8. Gun Hill, Southwold	11.5" x 9"
9. The Swan Hotel, Southwold	11" x 9"
10. The Sole Bay Inn, Southwold	10" x 8.25"
11. The Seafront, Kessingland	12" x 10"
12. St. Andrews at Covehithe	12" x 10"
13. Sea View path, Pakefield	16" x 11"
14. The Claremont Pier, Lowestoft	10" x 8"
15. Royal Norfolk and Suffolk Yacht Club And South Pier	4" x 8"
16. Lowestoft Inner Harbour	12.5" x 6.5"
17. Corton Beach	14" x 12"
18. Hopton Clifftop and Potter's Leisure Resort	15" x 12"
19. Lighthouse and Harbour, Gorleston	26" x 9"
20. Gorleston Beach and Pier	20" x 7"
21. The Hippodrome, Great Yarmouth	15" x 12"
22. Nelson's Column, Great Yarmouth	9" x 14"
23. Haven River Crossing, Great Yarmouth	20" x 10"
24. Anna Sewell's House, Great Yarmouth	8" x 10"
25. Caister Beach	10.5" x 10.5"
26. Caister Lifeboat Station	10" x 8"
27. Scratby Marrams	14" x 9"
28. Hemsby Sand Dunes	15" x 10"
29. Winterton Clifftop	20" x12"
30. Waxham Great Barn and Hall	24" x 10"
31. The Dunes, Waxham	18" x 12"
32. Beach Road, Sea Palling	10.5" x 10.5"
33. Cart Gap Boats, Eccles	16" x 8"
34. Happisburgh from lane	16" x 8"
35. Happisburgh Lighthouse	12" x 15"
36. Ostend	16" x 11"
37. Walcot	16" x 11"
38. Bacton	18" x 12"
39. Paston Great Barn	12" x 8"
40. Mundesley Stow Mill	8.75" x 7"
41. Coal Slipway, Mundesley	15" x 12"
42. Vale view road, Mundesley	10.5" x 10.5"
43. Trimingham	11" x 9"
44. Hungry Hill, Sidestrand	16" x 6"
45. The House in the Clouds, Thorpeness	11.5" x 9"
46. Sizewell Village	20" x 8"
47. Minsmere	24" x 12"
48. Tower Lane, Sidestrand	20" x 8"
49. Clifftop Café, Overstrand	18" x12"
50. Cromer Lighthouse	20" x 8"
51. Cromer East Beach	24" x 12"
52. Cromer Gangway and Lifeboat Café	12" x 15"
53. Cliff Study, East Runton	16" x 12"
54. Cliff Study, West Runton	16" x 12"
55. Beeston Regis Hill	14" x 12"
56. The Promenade, Sheringham	14" x 12"
57. Weybourne Cliffs	12" x 6"
58. Coast Road, Salthouse	20" x 8"
59. Kelling	11" x 9"
60. Cley	16" x 6"
61. Blakeney	15" x 12"
62. Blakeney Point	11.5" x 9
63. Morston Creek	20" x 8"
64. Stiffkey Red Lion	11.5" x 9"
65. Wells Quayside	10" x 8"
66. Holkham Bay	20" x 8"
67. Burnham Overy Staithe	20" x 6"
68. Burnham Norton Cottages	12" x 10"
69. Burnham Deepdale	10" x 8"
70. Brancaster Staithe	9" x 7"
71. Brancaster Beach	20" x 8"
72. Titchwell Village	10" x 8"
73. Thornham	20" x 8"
74. Holme-next-the-sea	16" x 6"
75. Old Hunstanton	10" x 8"
76. Hunstanton	10" x 8"
77. Heacham Lavander Farm	15" x 10"
78. Snettisham Beach	16" x 6"
79. Dersingham	15" x 10"
80. The Royal Station, Wolterton	14" x 11"
81. Sandringham House	16" x 11"
82. Castle Rising	14" x 8"
83. The South Gate, Kings Lynn	11.5" x 9"
84. The Customs House, Kings Lynn	12" x 10"

Map

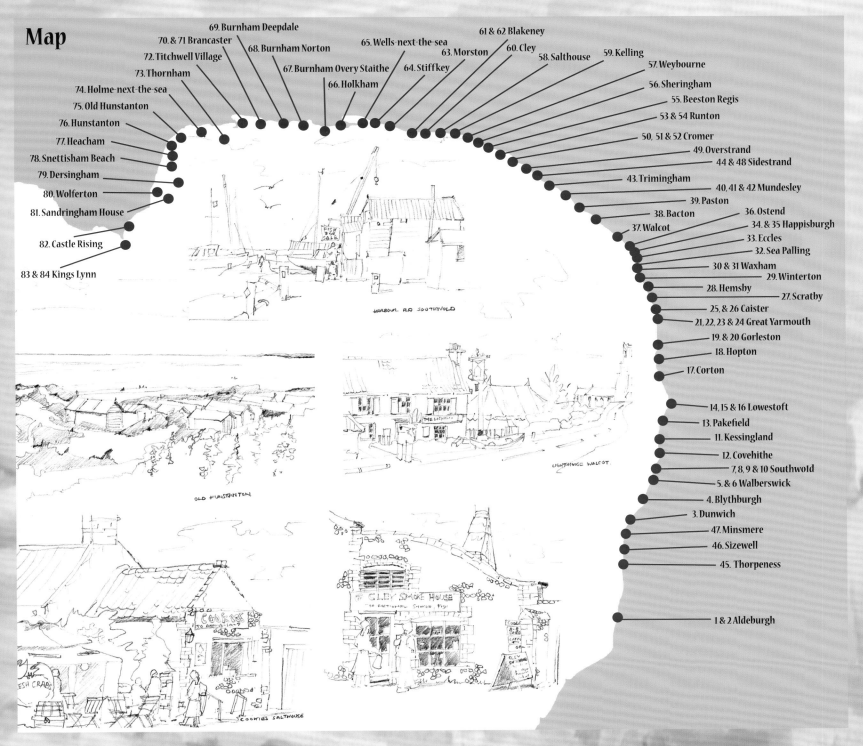

69. Burnham Deepdale
70. & 71 Brancaster
72. Titchwell Village
73. Thornham
74. Holme-next-the-sea
75. Old Hunstanton
76. Hunstanton
77. Heacham
78. Snettisham Beach
79. Dersingham
80. Wolferton
81. Sandringham House
82. Castle Rising
83 & 84 Kings Lynn

68. Burnham Norton
67. Burnham Overy Staithe
66. Holkham

65. Wells-next-the-sea
64. Stiffkey
63. Morston
60. Cley

61 & 62 Blakeney
58. Salthouse
59. Kelling
57. Weybourne
56. Sheringham
55. Beeston Regis
53 & 54 Runton
50, 51 & 52 Cromer
49. Overstrand
44 & 48 Sidestrand
43. Trimingham
40, 41 & 42 Mundesley
39. Paston
38. Bacton
37. Walcot
36. Ostend
34. & 35 Happisburgh
33. Eccles
32. Sea Palling
30 & 31 Waxham
29. Winterton
28. Hemsby
27. Scratby
25, & 26 Caister
21, 22, 23 & 24 Great Yarmouth
19. & 20 Gorleston
18. Hopton
17. Corton
14, 15 & 16 Lowestoft
13. Pakefield
11. Kessingland
12. Covehithe
7, 8, 9 & 10 Southwold
5. & 6 Walberswick
4. Blythburgh
3. Dunwich
47. Minsmere
46. Sizewell
45. Thorpeness
1 & 2 Aldeburgh

HARBOUR RD SOUTHWOLD

OLD HUNSTANTON

LIGHTHOUSE WALCOT.

COOKIES SALTHOUSE

GLEY SMOKE HOUSE

11

Monday 11th August 2008

1. Fresh Fish Aldeburgh

Oil 11.5"x9""

Location: Seafront Aldeburgh, North end of town facing the sea.

Weather: Warm but rather cloudy with very little breeze. Some sunny spells after midday.

Comments: Often when arriving in a town or location you are not over familiar with, the first subject that takes your eye is often the best picture to start. I was attracted by the juxtaposition of the fish shed, black and stark against the shingle bank with a rather green sea and sky back drop. I started about 10am and this seemed a good time to start

painting as his fresh fish catch was being landed, and there was a constant tooing and froing of locals for me to focus on. There were some delightful people to talk to and I spoke to Heather Maybey, formerly of Norwich and she remembered my gallery and framers in Orford Yard, all those years ago; and she remembered Michael Brett who has moved part of Looses into my old premises.

Various holiday makers commented on the painting, a nice couple staying in Felixstowe, who are not happy with their accommodation; and a man from Cambridge who stays regularly in Aldeburgh; and a keen twitcher who visits Minsmere often. After the painting was completed I relocated to the Moot Hall close by.

1 Fresh Fish Aldeburgh

Monday 11th August 2008

2. The Moot Hall

Oil 11"x9"

Location: It was rather silly of me but I started to paint in the road as the traffic was slight, but I had to move twice to allow adjacent parked cars to exit.

Weather: Weather: Warm but rather cloudy with very little breeze. Some sunny spells after midday.

Comments: This timber framed building is stunning and I believe was originally built for the local council where trade was conducted in medieval times. I don't suppose I did it justice but tried to give an impression of scale and its delicate timber framing. Later on I visited the museum inside, and learnt something about Aldeburgh and the coastal village close by lost to the sea in 1935. Things don't change much today with our threatened coastline. Amongst the displays were a small collection of etchings and watercolours by Martin Hardie, an early 20th century artist I particularly admire.

Further along the seafront are two imposing towers with small buildings adjacent that cling to the shingle bank. One is occupied by 'Coastline Picture Framing' whose owner is proud that he is England's most easterly picture frame maker, whatever they may say differently at Lowestoft! I immediately recognised the building from Peggy Somerville's painting, entitled 'Summer Aldeburgh'. Peggy was known as a child prodigy in the early 1900's, and held her first show in London at the age of 10. A delightful impressionistic artist whose work I much admire. Small exhibitions of her paintings can be seen at 'Messums Fine Art' in Cork Street from time to time.

I cannot go without mentioning Mary Potter, who had various studios and houses on the seafront, and was perhaps one of Aldeburgh's most celebrated female artists.

I left Aldeburgh about 4pm, regretting not having enough time to visit the yacht' club, bringing back happy memories of sailing with the Chadd family on their vintage yacht 'The Rosemary'. Perhaps another time. Note should also be made of the magnificent but controversial shell sculpture by Maggie Hamling standing proud on the shingle bank. She once was a pupil of Cedric Morris at Barton End, going on to become one of England's most important female painters. I believe she lives in the Aldeburgh area.

Last and perhaps not least, I take away the memory of the little bronze statue of a dog named 'Snooks' who stands on a plinth by the yacht pond, dedicated to his Doctor owners memory. Most charming.

2. The Moot Hall

3. The Flora Tea Rooms and beach Dunwich
Oil 14"x10"

Location: I painted adjacent to he Tea Rooms a few yards down the shingle bank, looking towards Sizewell Power station.

Weather: Bright sunshine with scudding cotton wool clouds- Became quite breezy by lunchtime when rain stopped play.

Comments: Because Christine made an early start to interior clients in Bedford, I found myself at Dunwich by 9am. The sun was on my left giving the sea its sparkling reflection. I'm not used to this as round the corner, as they say in Norfolk, reflected sun on water can usually only be seen up at Hunstanton because of the angle of the coastline. I had the beach virtually to myself, apart from a brave middle aged couple taking a dip. Hardy types as they stayed in at least 20 minutes, swimming up and down in the rollers and breakers. Painting continued unabated apart from talking to a couple from Essex who took my photo promising to send it on to me by email. On completion I went in the tea rooms for coffee and was staggered by the number of tables ready for their renowned fish and chip lunches. The staff told me how hundreds of cyclists annually make a trip in July coming up from London on a charity run.

The tea rooms themselves have been here from Victorian times and still survive despite a major fire in 1987. The present owner has been here for at least 20 years. On returning home I called in for lunch at  The Ship Inn, yum yum! One of the perks of being a starving artist. Next door was the museum featuring the history of Dunwich. And the paintings by Edward T Lingwood caught my eye. Various scenes of coastal erosion with the demise of All saints Church. The village itself was once owned by the Barnes family in the 19th century and had been architecturally styled in the Tudor period. Latticed windows, Tudor chimneys and fleur de leys decorated tile work.

I eventually made my way home crossing the forested Dunwich heath and by the back roads to Blythburgh. Many artists have been touched by the drama and romanticism of Dunwich and its hinterland. From Piper to Ivon Hitchens in the 1930's. The latter was featured at Narborough hall in 2007 and Piper in 2008. A stunning location for exhibitions of this quality and of which East Anglians should be justly proud.

JILL ANNE   oDUNWICH

3. The Flora Tea Rooms and Beach Dunwich

Thursday 14th August 2008
4. The White Hart, Blythburgh

Oil 11.5"x9"

Location: I stood on the pavement on the very bad bend at Blythburgh. The White Hart was opposite with the Blyth estuary behind the pub. Heavy traffic was literally at my elbow.

Weather: Hot and very close with the occasional cloud. Rain was forecast by lunchtime but didn't materialise.

Comments: The White Hart as subject matter for me was really a trip down memory lane as I spent many a happy evening in there with the landlord and his son. The son was recovering from illness after serving in Belize with the army where he was taken ill and invalided out into civvy street. I believe he is making a good life working as a freelance photographer. I spoke to the present manager who said that the building dated back to the 15th century, and was used at one time as a courthouse. a tunnel exists under the road to a cottage next to where I was painting, bricked up now no doubt. The pub itself had an eclectic collection of customers. Most of them good Boule players,

a game which I became interested in but never quite mastered. One chap, Ray, was an artist/illustrator who had a studio over the garage of one of the finest timber houses in Blythburgh. His work was quite unique, as he had to illustrate in watercolour, the cover of dress making patterns that people received. All he had to go on was a few swatches through the post with the pattern details and had to turn them all in to inviting images. A truly remarkable talent.

I remember playing boule in the pub grounds which looked out on to the beautiful Blyth estuary. On the other side of the road stands the magnificent Blythburgh Church. Home to that legend of these parts- Black Shuck. The legendary demon possessed dog who ran a mock in the church, terrorising and killing the congregation. He is said to still stalk these parts at night. I rented Rose Cottage there for some months but managed to avoid him! It is possible to walk from across the road along the line of the old narrow guage railway, now removed to Walberswick. The route takes you through the pine woods on the banks of the Blyth estuary, and would have carried a whole host of artists who colonised Walberswick in the late 19th century. Charles Rennie Mackintosh and Phillip Wilson Steer, no doubt took this route. I don't know if the White Hart was a pub then, but just two weeks ago Charles and Camilla (Windsor), stopped by for a drink and to support the local shop and post office on their way to Adnams brewery at Southwold. My next painting trip will be to Walberswick but sadly not on the old twig and branch line. Just one person spoke to me whilst painting, who was a young polish girl living with her artist partner in the village so we swapped yarns of how difficult it is to make a living and talked about Mary Gundry, an artist who lives close by whom I exhibited with at one time when she had the garden gallery in Southwold.

4. The White Hart Blythburgh

Tuesday 26th August 2008

5. By the Blyth, Walberswick

Oil 16"x11"

Location: Adjacent to the slipway in the lee of the old wooden clad buildings by the Blyth river.

Weather: Very warm and humid as I set off and it stayed like that most of the day. A few sunny spells broke through as the day progressed.

Comments: as usual when arriving, in a picturesque spot I spent too much time wandering around to find a good space to paint so to speak. I can't think why as I know and have painted here several times over the years. It was slightly windy so stood in the lee of holiday cottages facing down the Blyth with the slipway in the foreground, and the old wooden jetty used by the ferry woman in the mid distance. It was high tide on arrival and watched a flashy plastic boat coming to moorings together with a large inflatable rib boat for carrying trippers out to sea. It looked great fun. Technically the painting was quite easy, but struggled a bit with changing light conditions. Subsequently the painting had a rather cool grey tonal quality.

Robert Horsfall, a passing cyclist, kindly took my photograph for future reference. The lady holidaying in the cottage next to me stopped to say hi, together with a woman in a floppy hat who was a keen artist. Neither mentioned my painting but talked about their own work mostly. That's human nature I suppose. The scene in front of me which was initially quite deserted, gradually started apace filling with happy families, line dipping for crabs on the slipway and riverbank. Quite colourful. It was soon time to pack up and sat with my feet dangling over the

river bank whilst I ate sandwiches and pop. It was almost as if I was on holiday too! Well must crack on as there was still enough time left to paint one more picture so headed over to the kissing bridge to the beach. This bridge was much painted by artists including Wilson Steer. I had myself an etching by H J Starling incidently of the same view.

5. By the Blyth, Walberswick

6. The Beach, Walberswick
Oil 12"x10"

Comments: The beach itself was quite busy but most holiday makers were well wrapped up and sat behind their wind breaks. The painting was like old times, as it depicted the old lifeboat house which was removed by crane from the end of Cromer Pier, and transported by barge to rest at the end of the Blyth Estuary on the Southwold bank. It is now used as a maritime museum, I believe.

Walberswick was quickly colonised by artists in the 19th century, attracted to the old village warmly welcomed by villagers in those days. Glad to offer cheap accommodation to supplement their meagre income, earned mainly by hard toil on the land, or by landing fish from small boats. Phillip Wilson Steer painted here and perhaps in the publics' eyes was best known for his pictures of children paddling and knuckle bones . Both I believe were exhibited at Norwich Castle Museum and Art Gallery quite recently. Charles Rennie Mackintosh, an artist who rests deep in my heart, for both his artistic brilliance and architectural buildings, many of which I have seen on frequent visits to Glasgow, also resided here. Alas his stay was not to be a happy sojourn here as he was accused of being an enemy spy. Actually Mackintosh frequently corresponded with clients in Austria as he struggled to find commissions for his designs. Not a sensible thing to do in wartorn Europe, at a time of impending war.

Last but not least, I should like to mention Margaret Mellis, one time seduced by Walberswick, but settling with her first husband Adrian Stokes eventually in Cornwall. One can well imagine her working alongside Barbara Hepworth and Ben Nicholson during the second world war years. Luckily for us Margaret returned to East Anglia and married her second husband Francis Davidson.

The Sainsbury Centre For Visual Arts in Norwich put on a magnificent show of her work with quite large constructions in scale, made from flotsam and jetsam found no doubt on the foreshore at Walberswick. If you looked carefully broken bits of ribs of boats could be seen cleverly pieced together to form engaging compositions. Called at the Bell Inn and had a light ale, a drink gone out of favour but happily making a return. Walberswick's most famous resident artist being William Bowyer RA who I am indebted to for selecting one of my paintings to show at the Castle Museum in an open art show this coming October.

Patrick Burrell

6. The Beach, Walberswick

Thursday 28th August 2008

7. Gun Hill Café Southwold

Oil 16"x12

Location: Behind the beach huts adjacent to the Gun Hill Café, with the slipway and promenade in the foreground.

Weather: Once again hot and sultry with overcast skies threatening rain but cleared by midday and became quite sunny. There was a fairly fresh breeze coming off the land.

Comments: I had a very frazzled start to the day as I had to pass by my picture framer Peter Richardson with some of my signed prints on route to Southwold, which should have meant going via Harleston and Halesworth. I got incredibly lost and knew this when I saw a sign to 'Oasis Camel Centre'! Surely I wasn't in North Africa already! East Coast would do! Suffice to say I eventually arrived having seen parts of Suffolk hitherto unknown to me. I parked in the south end of town on the road leading to Black Water Quay and climbed over the dunes to the Gun Hill Café. It was fairly breezy so painted between dunes and beach huts and got on quite well considering my journey. As ever with

painting with a dull sky I had to change my picture to allow for the brightening skies that came later. This is a very busy spot, ideal if you want to add figures to a picture. Spoke to quite a lot of people, getting one man to take my photo for future reference. A member of Southwold art circle liked my picture, and offered his estimate of sale price. I don't think he realised an artist has to give up nearly 50 per cent of commission these days to a good gallery. Taking off the framing costs it would make a small reward for so much effort. Books galore have been written on Southwold and its surroundings, very much the grand sister compared with Walberswick.

The Gun Hill Café subject I particularly liked having seen aHugo Grenville's painting of the same in David Messums old St James' street gallery many years ago. He is the artist known for setting fire to all his old paintings in a fit of despair but thankfully carried on again when he had revaluated the way forward.

7. Gun Hill Café Southwold

Thursday 28th August 2008

8. Gun Hill

Oil 11.5" x 9".

Comments: After a cup of tea from the café, and a hurried snack, I climbed up the coastal path to Gun Hill and looked back at the canons and the magnificent panorama of Sole Bay with Dunwich and Sizewell in the far distance. Apparently legend has it the canons were given to the town by the Duke of Cumberland, after a battle with Bonnie Prince Charlie's men as he stopped over. By now the scene was bathed in sunshine and I was able to capture parents and kids clambering over the canons, a scene that must have been repeated over the generations. I know my girls Natalie and Sophie did exactly the same. A plethora of artists have been attracted to the town most notably Stanley Spencer's painting of the beach and wind breaks comes to mind; Bertram Priestman who encouraged a young Edward Seago and not to forget Joseph Southalls paintings on silk. I have only seen a few since included in an exhibition at the Castle Museum and Art Gallery, perhaps my favourite of his work I saw at the Burrell Collection in Glasgow.

End of a very tiring day but to do justice to Southwold I envisaged returning, weather permitting. (By the way Southwold District Council, the toilets closed by the beach in the height of summer could cause panic in an old man like me!).

8. Gun Hill

Friday 29th August 2008

9. The Swan Hotel, Southwold

Oil 11"x9"

Location: Painted adjacent to Ann Brewster's shop on the high street with a view of The Swan opposite. The girls in the shop gave me permission. Ann was an old customer of mine years back when I had our garden furniture business.

Weather: Today was very hot and humid and threatened rain at times but kept breaking out in sunshine. Very little wind..

Comments: : Several people who had passed me by from yesterday came for another look today. Must be gluttons for punishment. Southwold was very busy so I was glad to be standing in my little back water.

Peter Gibbs, an antique dealer in Southwold, came to say hello and invited me for coffee later. We reminisced about old times when he ran 'The Room With A View' art gallery in St Benedict's, Norwich and hung a few of my pictures from time to time. We talked about how Mary Gundry and I used to have joint exhibitions in the large room at the back of The Sutherland House Restaurant. She later went on to start her own gallery in the High Street, subsequently selling the gallery to a local artist.

HARBOUR RD SOUTHWOLD

9. The Swan Hotel, Southwold

Tuesday 26th August 2008

10. The Sole Bay Inn

Oil 10" x 8.25"

Comments: By lunchtime I had finished a quite complicated picture in so far as its' architecture was concerned, so I then went on to paint the Sole Bay Inn with its distant view of the sea. The pub was packed out giving me ample opportunity to paint customers coming and going. Met some very nice people from London who asked where I exhibited at the moment and gave me lots of compliments which was nice. I thought I would get a sandwich from the Bay which came in an enormous portion, even for a gannet like me! Shouldn't complain. I liked the photographs and lifebelt of HMS Sole Bay decorating the pub, and the landlord informed me it was decommissioned in 1964 and either sold or broken up, no doubt. After packing up I bumped into Robert and Victoria Plumbly, customers of mine who chose a nice painting for his retirement from councillor duties. They have subsequently bought one of Brancaster golf club. They said they owned a house in Southwold which made me green with envy. Two days of painting here really is not enough to do justice to the place. However, I am returning next month for the wedding at the Swan Hotel of Tom and Rhiannon Mead – to- be, and afterwards a knees up a the Harbour Inn. Perhaps I'll get time to do another painting then as I am staying with the wedding party in a cottage close by.

CROWN HOTEL SOUTHWOLD

10. The Sole Bay Inn

Monday 1st September 2008

11. The Sea Front Kessingland

Oil 12"x10"

Location: On the Promenade at Kessingland just north of the Waterfront Cafe

Weather: A really bright warm day after the thunderstorm of Sunday. Small clouds scudding across the sky. Rain threatened by lunch time as predicted.

Comments: Kessingland is a place I have only visited once before. It epitomises all that I remember of childhood holidays with beach cafes, local pubs and very little else to distract. I stood on the promenade with the wide shingled beach to my left constantly changing as the clouds crossed the sky. To my right was a steep bank where a soon to be erected 'Huff House' or similar, would have commanding views of the ocean. A really superb site it would be built by Taylors of nearby Reydon with the main contractors TAVO MAMMAS who are Lithuanian. This will be an amazing building to be placed so close to other older and more traditional sea side cottages. Well done planners in giving it the go ahead. I digress a little as architecture in the landscape is very much

my thing. There were some jolly local people came by as I painted. An old man, a Mr Blowers whose family, father, and grandfather have been fishermen off this coast. He could trace his ancestry back 250 years.

A short while later I spoke to the landlord of the pub, The Sailors, a Mr Poppy who himself is a keen fisherman. He talked about a fisherman who had just left the pub who had lost his boat at sea and had spent two and a half hours in the water before being picked up. He was a very lucky man. The Landlord told me he had a boat called 'Twin Boys' named after his two grandchildren and recently bought in Northern Ireland. My work was done here and I was inspired by a passer by to visit Benacre, slightly south of Kessingland. Unfortunately I could not find it but travelled through some beautiful countryside and was struck by the immaculate condition of the thatched barns and agricultural buildings on the Benacre estate. Eventually, with my access blocked by too many private estate roads, I ended up in Covehithe, a small village unknown to me before.

The St Andrews Church stands proud amidst its ruined predecessor gradually being restored, together with its finely tuned bells. The road once again was private though I could have possibly proceeded on foot which could have been difficult with all my equipment. I should really have painted a picture of the church in ruins as I approached from the Wrentham direction. A pity really as the expected rainfall had not materialised as I sped homeward. Oh well, lets see what tomorrow brings.

Boswells Coast

11. The Sea Front Kessingland

12. St Andrews at Covehithe

Oil 12"x10"

Location: : At first thought I debated whether to paint the church on its approach from Wrentham but settled in the end on its other approaching side.

Weather: Dull start to the day but by mid morning the skies cleared and I was cooled by a fresh south westerly

Comments: I parked my car next to the church and proceeded on foot to find a suitable gateway to assemble my equipment. It was quite glorious with the sun beating down on my left hand side and to the right a field of gentle snuffling pigs. This area, known for its wildlife' certainly lived up to it here with flocks of geese rising, precipitated by crop guns. Bird song in the hedgerows accompanied my labours and I was soon lost in the atmosphere of the place. Only one car and a man on a bike passed by in several hours with just a good old East Anglian nod of the head. Nearly said Norfolk then. I keep forgetting I am so far from home and lost in the beautiful countryside around here. Funnily enough on radio Suffolk it mentioned St Andrews that morning as a place that might be lost to the sea. The cliffs are literally only a few hundred yards down the road which are blocked off due to the precarious nature of the terrain. By the by I have just seen a stoat or was it a weasel, pass literally within a few feet of me. Answers on a postcard please.

13. Seaview path, Pakefield

Oil 16"x11"

Comments: There was still a good moment in the day and I found myself by the large All Saints Parish Church with its' double hipped roof of thatch perched precariously on the cliff top path. I had a commanding view of the shingle beach below and the sweep of the bay extending to Kessingland southwards in the far distance. My subject of beach and boats is one I am familiar with as I painted it twice before at beach level with the boats close up. Ever a popular subject I have seen paintings of the same view by Ian Houston, Edward Seago and Arnesby Brown all making fabulous attempts at this great subject. The latter I was privileged to see in David Messum's gallery and discuss with him its museum quality. I expect as a hard nosed business gallery owner it did not stay in his hands long.

A few passers by said "Good Day" but continued on their dog walking ways. Quite a peaceful scene disturbed only by the screech of seagulls overhead and the clarion calls of Mr Lamarti's ice cream van stopping close by. Pakefield has a certain faded elegance about it in contrast to its close by sister town, Lowestoft. I asked a local if they could identify where one started and the other finished without too much success. On packing up my equipment, a group of horses with disabled riders came by followed later by a woman shovelling up their residue as they passed, into plastic bags. "Too good an opportunity" she remarked ,for her garden.

Because I was painting into the sun coupled with the fresh breeze speed was of the essence and I broke down the subject matter into blocks of colour. The sea was ever changing with deep shadows cast horizontally across the shore.

Friday 5th September 2008

14. Claremont Pier Lowestoft

Oil 10"x 8"

Location: On the promenade adjacent to the ogee roofed tourist information centre with its toilet and café.

Weather: A very dull day which brightened occasionally but as usual the sun did not appear until after I was on my way home

Comments: : I was facing southwards with the line of the breakwaters interspersing my picture with the Claremont Pier in the distance.

It was very dull so I must admit I cheated a bit and put in a bright and breezy sky as otherwise the whole scene would have been in very muted tones. It was a little cold to start with but was able to chat to an occasional holiday maker who seemed to be from York or Derbyshire perhaps, talking about the terrible floods in their home county.

Though East Anglia is relatively flat, flooding is for the most part very localised with the exception of course with major breaches of flood defences back in the 1950's

14. Claremont Pier Lowestoft

Friday 5th September 2008

15. The Royal Norfolk & Suffolk Yacht Club with South Pier Pavilion

Oil 24" x 8"

Location: On the promenade adjacent to the ogee roofed tourist information centre with its toilet and café.

Weather: A very dull day which brightened occasionally but as usual the sun did not appear until after I was on my way home.

Comments: The Claremont picture was soon finished so after a quick bite to eat I turned my attention to the Yacht Club, a building that I am quite familiar with as my father was once a member, keeping his MV boat 'Sea Girl' on a mooring there. I, at one time, sailed with Dr. David Boswell, my father's cousin of Oulton Broad in his Broads One Design. He was an active member of the club. I crewed with his daughter Sarah, who I have lost contact with over the years.

As I looked to the right of the scene that I was painting, I well remember racing my old enterprise number 640 'Zuleika' offshore at the clubs' Summer Regatta ably crewed at times by Peter Tacon and Richard Fairburns. I remember, in one race, coming close inshore because of the tide, a Dragon class boat had run aground and the crew were ordered over the side to push off. Unfortunately, they were too short so the helmsman jumped in himself. Thankfully, he was very tall and turned out to be a consultant heart surgeon at the Norfolk and Norwich Hospital, Mr Oliver. Happy times.

My father and I, quite often took his boat over to Holland for our annual holidays. This brought back memories of a painting trip I took a few years ago to Enhuisen, Horn and other Isselmeer towns that have beautiful scenery, just like Norfolk.

Whilst painting I spoke to literally loads of holiday makers and, I think, a lot of them were from the North of England and were very friendly, perhaps a little too much as I had trouble finishing my work. Surprisingly, I spoke to Richard Mead, the father of my daughter Natalie's boyfriend James. We had a long chat about the coast and found out that

he lives quite close to the 'Huff House' I described earlier. His other son, Tom, is getting married at The Swan at Southwold so I will see him again in about a fortnight. It's a small world, Norfolk.

The painting itself was initially a bit out of control but I concentrated on the central part in particular so I managed to pull the whole thing together. Some woman said "Ee that's right good." I think she was from Derbyshire, who would have guessed! PS I have just been attacked by horrid storm flies and it is going to take some serious de-flying on the wet paint when I get home!

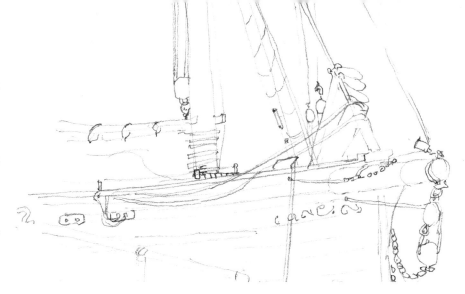

15. The Royal Norfolk & Suffolk Yacht Club with South Pier Pavilion

Tuesday September 9th 2008

16. Lowestoft Inner Harbour

Oil 16"x11"

Location: Painted on pavement looking toward the Pier heads marking the harbour wall

Weather: What a difference a day makes, grey skies with a smattering of rain. A strong south easterly was blowing on shore.

Comments:: Today was going to be one of those days as although I had arrived with plenty of time I only had enough change for three hours on the public car park. I decided to paint the inner harbour area which was enclosed by security fencing and after talking to a nice man in charge of bridge building operations he said I would have to ask at the little hut leading to the harbour area and he would ring ahead and assured me that permission would just be a formality. The end result was, after trekking a considerably long way with my equipment the hut man telephoned his boss who passed permission on to his second in command who refused although I was prepared to sign forms of indemnity. What a palaver. The harbour is completely empty apart form one tug and the area is crying out for development with good harbour access for the public. Heavy rain was forecast later so I was under some pressure to finish. The painting took on very grey and silvery tones because of the light but nonetheless was not too Ken Howardish as a result, Few people stopped apart from a friendly community police office commenting on my painting through the bars of the harbour railings. The harbour road I was on still had echoes of its past glories. Buildings had names such as Columbus House, The Colne Shipping Company, The Seaman's Rescue and perhaps the most indicative, The Good Rock Rope Company. I well remember this same spot being the subject of a painting commissioned by my sister for her

dining room in the sixties by H E Collins, of trawlers and drifters crammed in here. How times have changed. Lowestoft itself was frequented by many young artists of the 20th Century. Geoffrey Chatten, Roland Fisher and the young Edward Sego more famously painted pictures of the Royal Norfolk and Suffolk Yacht Club which hang today proudly on the walls of this fine establishment.

Appropriate really as he was a friend of the Duke of Edinbugh, himself the clubs' patron. Seago's boat, The Endeavour, was to be lost itself on the shores of this coast. I worked myself, in my youth, as a GRP Laminator on Wapload Road opposite the old Birds Eye factory for Lancer Marine manufacturing high performance speed boats. The firm had its' assembly factory at nearby Oulton Broad but went bust in spectacular fashion with creditors who had made staged payments for their boats breaking into the factory in the days leading up to its collapse. Later on in my life, having started an art and faming business, I was privileged to clean and reframe many of the marine paintings displayed at the Sparrows Nest Museum. Luckily, after a fire the damage was relatively small and was soon rectified. They have some lovely local Victorian paintings by Burwood amongst others. Of special interest to me are

the Pier head paintings framed in little lifebelts of about 10″ in diameter . These were undertaken often in a lively style by sailors to supplement their income. Many have survived to this day as the owners hung them on the bulk heads of their boats. A lovely museum well worth a visit. I could not leave without a visit to Ness Point, the most easterly place in England. A bit disappointing really because it is part of an industrial estate. I liked the circular pavement display telling you the distance to various parts of the world. Rotterdam 122 miles, Amsterdam 132 miles and Ostend at 101 miles being our nearest destination from this point. Just time to do a quick drawing and head for home. Tomorrow Corton , I wonder what that is like?

Wednesday September 10th

17. Corton Beach

Oil 16"x11"

Location: Beach Road, Corton.

Weather: A very sunny day with a light, onshore breeze and with a few broken clouds. As the day progressed the wind built up to quite a strength creating some heavy dark clouds.

Comments: What a difference a day makes as I set up my easel adjacent to the beach car park. This is entered through heavy concrete blocks with arrows stating the gap is 6' 6". Not for the faint hearted to be passed at speed. I had the beach to myself for most of the time with just a few fishermen on the beach. They were quite friendly but like the old fishermen's tale 'it was always better the day before'. Apparently they have a conspiracy theory that inshore trawlermen are laying ropes to snag their tackle and to stop them taking their stock. Doesn't sound plausible really.

The scene was stunning in the sunlight with Yarmouth and Hopton in the distance. To my left at the top of the cliffs was a row of houses with superb views of the sea. What a place to live with access to the beach at your doorstep.

I was quite pleased with my painting although I had the sun shining directly on to my palette which did not help. Mustn't grumble. Just before leaving I spoke briefly to a young man who painted aircraft at Norwich airport. He had been up until 2.00 in the morning working on an RAF plane.

You never can judge what people do these days. He is off for a few days fishing but I do not envy him working all day long with a face mask on.

42

17. Corton Beach

18. Hopton Cliff Top and Potter's Leisure Resort

Oil 15" x 12"

Comments: Having finished at Corton I spent some time looking for Hopton and eventually found it tucked away off the main A12 to Yarmouth road. I came across Potter's Leisure Centre and a very nice lady in a senior management position gave me permission to go on to their property. It is the fist time that I have been here since my parents brought us on a family holiday just after the war. 'What a difference' would be an understatement.

The leisure facilities indeed looked second to none and have deservedly won them national recognition for their indoor bowling competitions that they stage there.

On finding the cliff top spot that I was looking for it was quite some distance from the car park, I therefore decided to drive down the side of Potters where the public have access to the beach. A great scene with the beach, cliffs and breakwaters stretching into the distance towards Ness Point. Potters with the Millenium beacon was to my right.

I am getting quite used to painting these as they occur all along the coast.

18. Hopton Cliff Top and Potter's Leisure Report

Monday 15th September 2008

19. Lighthouse and Harbour Entrance, Gorleston

Oil 26" x 9"

Location: On the raised sea wall with the river on my left, lighthouse and tower in the mid distance.

Weather: A lovely sunny day with a light breeze blowing directly on shore. Not at all cold for the time of year.

Comments: I was fortunate today to be joined by my friend and fellow artist, Paul Darley. I picked him up from Norwich Station before 9.00am and we were soon in Gorleston. We soon found a suitable place by the river. Gorleston has been painted by Paul many times over the years as he, at one time did assistant stage management work at The Pavillion Theatre, just visible in my painting. This same view has attracted artists such as Edward Seago and Rowland Fisher. Fisher lived high up on Cliff Avenue and had a commanding view of this scene.

The sun was ahead of me and made the river sparkle and put figures and town in sharp silhouette. I chose an elongated landscape board for my painting as it suited the subject best.

By late morning we had both finished and Paul did a lovely picture of the river with projecting quay headings. Quite stunning. He, in fact, managed another facing a similar direction to myself with fishermen on the quay complementing the composition. Coffee was called for and we packed up momentarily to a small café opposite the Pier Hotel and the Ocean Rooms. The latter, I well remember as a boy, being the venue for our swimming gala, for Langley School in those days. My only success was in the maximum distance swim in the underwater competition, though I probably nearly went blue in the face attempting this.

19. Lighthouse and Harbour Entrance, Gorleston

20. Gorleston Beach and Pier

Oil 20" x 7"

Comments: After stopping for a quick bite to eat we de-camped to the other side of the Pier Hotel where the sand sweeps in a natural bay from the harbour jetty. Campbell Mellon of Gorleston fame pretty well made this his own scene with crowds of holiday makers crammed into every square inch of canvas. For my part the beach was practically empty but the simplicity of this gave a few foreground figures much dramatic effect. The sun this time was from behind but my shadow on the palette helped in mixing my colours.

20. Gorleston Beach and Pier

Paul too had finished a rather nice pier head picture from further along the promenade. We departed Gorleston by 4.00pm well satisfied by our days' efforts. I think, sometimes having a painting companion can spur you on to make that extra effort. Paul said he might join me again. Let's hope so.

Tuesday 16th September 2008

21. The Hippodrome, Great Yarmouth

Oil 15" x 12"

Location: Adjacent to The Golden Nugget Arcade, opposite The Hippodrome.

Weather: Quite dull and cloudy first thing but brightened as the day progressed. Sunny by lunchtime.

Comments: I chose The Hippodrome for my subject as it has always been a building that has fascinated me from a child with it's ornate buttresses and domed towers. The circus has been a magnet for artists from Edward Seago to Dame Laura Knight. The Hippodrome's ring can transform itself into a pool for swimming spectaculars and remains a delight for generations of people young and old alike.

I was privileged to talk to the owner's son who kept an eye on my progress. His father Peter, was at Norwich City College with me in the 60's. He formed a rock band in the basement for practise and eventually went on to front the Jaywalkers and featured as a supporting act to The Beatles.

The building is immensely complex and decorative so the picture took rather longer than anticipated, although I am glad that I attempted it. The manager in The Golden Nugget was very kind and gave me a cup of coffee whilst I worked and his staff were complimentary.

As the sun came out it was only a short walk to the beach where I sat and had my sandwiches. Yarmouth for a day visit is at its' best this time of year with not too many people. Talking to a few traders the season has not been that good unfortunately. Still, with the credit crunch at the moment maybe people will take their holidays at home in the future.

21. The Hippodrome, Great Yarmouth

Later that same day

22. Nelson's Column

Oil 14" x 9"

Comments: After a little time spent looking for the best viewpoint, quite difficult as the monument is surrounded on three sides by industrial buildings. Originally it stood magnificently in isolation amid the Naval paraphernalia of that time. Facing the river on one side and behind Brittania, the sea from whence he came. A few column facts; it stands

144 feet high with 217 steps to the top. It was designed by local architect William Wilkins who went on to design The National Gallery. Although some 5 metres shorter than its' London counterpart it makes up for it with architectural decoration. Those in the know , know what Coade Stone Finials, Caryatis, Drum, Abacus and Echines are. I am sure I don't.

Nelson, on receiving the Freedom Of Yarmouth was asked by the Mayor to take the oath in his right hand. Nelson replied "Sir, I cannot as I left it in Tenerife".

At any rate it was a fine structure to paint. It reminded me of my schooldays with the battles of Abukir, Copenhagen and Trafalgar all clearly inscribed on its' pediment. The architectural practice where my wife works, Purcell Miller Tritton, worked on the restoration of the column recently . At that height not a job for the faint hearted.

Surprisingly, in this isolated spot , a few holiday makers passed comment and moaned about how it was free the last time they came to climb to the top. Now I think £7.50 for all those steps . It would be a heart attack waiting to happen for me. No wonder your visit is restricted to 45 minutes, most of which would be to get your breath back. Enough said about a great subject. Let's hope Brittania may have her environment more exposed one day.

YARMOUTH QUAYSIDE.

22. Nelson's Column

53

Monday 22nd September 2008

23. The Haven River Crossing, Yarmouth

20" x 10"

Location: On the main bridge at Yarmouth with the Town Hall over to my left and the river stretching ahead.

Weather: A grey, overcast day threatening to rain. Changed completely by lunchtime with bright sunshine.

Comments: It was with leaden legs that I made my way to Yarmouth this morning after a day in London trekking around Decorex, Focus, 100% Design and Chelsea Harbour trade shows. Christine's bag carrier did her proud!

I parked up behind the old annexe to Yarmouth Art College which Christine went to. It's looking very forlorn now with boarded up windows. It was such a vibrant place hitherto. En route to the bridge I passed by Kevin Thompson's exhibitions at The Museum Galleries. It was quite a good show with over 120 pictures showing.

There was not much activity on the river but I was lucky to have two of the old clinker longshore boats in the foreground moored up, I expect from the previous Maritime weekend. This particular spot is a dangerous mooring as I remember Percy Percival from Horning who regularly went from Yarmouth to Ostend, left his private motor cruiser there one day and she was hit by a turning Harbour vessel which swept down towards the bridge on a strong tide, sinking her.

My painting position on the bridge could not have been more noisy and busy with what seemed like a continuous stream of ambulances and fire engines fighting their way through traffic with sirens blaring. It, at least, cut down my conversations with the locals and concentrated my efforts.

Before I conclude this extract on the Haven Bridge I must recall my two good Yarmouth friends, Malcolm Ferrow, who kindly let me hang some of my paintings in his beautiful antique

showrooms nearby. Also the lovely Harry Dyer who had his art supply and picture restoration business around the corner. He was ever ready to help with restoration tips from my picture dealing days . I was privileged to enter his rather shambolic

workshop to the rear of the shop. He had a very fine collection of 18th and 19th Century paintings built up over the years. Rumour has it that within 24 hours of his death they were transported to London for sale. So sad as they were his raison d'etre. Harry was sadly missed and was known to many a generation of Yarmouth Art College students, Christine included. Not the kind of shop to pop into for a quick purchase as Harry lived in a different world of relaxed conversation and a slower pace of life.

Later the same day

24. Anna Sewell House

Oil 10" x 8"

Comments: After lunch my parking ticket had run out so I drove to a car park near St. Nicholas Church and Anna Sewell House. I had originally intended to paint the old railway bridge crossing the river as the curved top shape would have made an interesting composition. This and the concrete road bridge have been the nemisis of many a Broads cruiser swept down on a strong tide with the end result of slamming into them. I well remember a holidaymaker throwing me his mooring line in an effort to save himself but attached to it was the rond anchor which flew past my head. No damage done and I managed to take him into tow safely from my Father's converted lifeboat, Rombo .

Sewell's house had always fascinated me. Reputedly the birthplace of Anna the authoress of Black Beauty, born March 30th 1820, it is now run as a very small restaurant by Richard Hughes, a well known chef who also runs The Lavender House at Brundall. Such a charming building, it was a pleasure to paint. For many years it was run as a café, I believe. Job done and I winged my way homewards.

Monday 29th September

25. Caister Beach

Oil 10.5 x 10.5"

Location: On the beach at the end of Beach Rd..

Weather: Very sunny and quite warm. Virtually no wind.

Comments: After a fabulous weekend in Southwold at the wedding of Tom and Rhiannon Mead, at The Swan Hotel, the weather held good and I found my way to Caister. It must be childhood since I was last on the beach when my father brought us up to the then Caister holiday camp for a lovely family holiday, just after the war. Virtually untouched since then, Caister still has a certain charm.

The sun was on my back for my first painting looking westwards towards Scratby, and it depicted old cottages nestling into the sand dunes with the sweep of the coast to the right in the distance. Quite a simple scene but I pulled it off effectively, I hope.

25. Caister Beach

Later the same day

26. Caister Lifeboat Station

Oil 10 x 8"

Comments: My second picture showed the edge of the Scroby Sands wind farm. Quite a sight as I hadn't seen them close up like this before. I painted directly into the sun with the sea sparkling before me speaking to virtually nobody all day, with just the occasional dog walker passing by. A lonely spot but I wonder what it's like in mid-summer. I didn't really have time to make a close inspection of the life boat house but was reminded of the life boatmen's motto " Caister men never turn back" as I passed a local pub, aptly named the same. After lunch at the Old Manor Café it was homeward bound via Ormesby and Filby feeling satisfied having two paintings completed.

26. Caister Lifeboat Station

Wednesday October 1st

27. Scratby Marrams

Oil 14 x 9"

Location: Low Road at Scratby, mid way between Scratby Marrams and Hemsby.

Weather: Temperature had dropped considerably and with strong winds made for a sunny but blustery environment.

Comments: My intention was to find the picturesque wooden cliff top buildings depicted by David Poole in his book " Norfolk Coastal Sketches" but they proved elusive. Eventually, after much directing by locals, I came upon a few still remaining reminiscent of holidays taken simply in those post war years. Their location could only be approached by car from the Hemsby direction when I found myself after much to-ing and fro-ing via caravan sites galore, came to it at last. These little buildings nestle against the dunes and are punctuated by electric and telegrah poles. EDF electricity providers had an army of lorries replacing lines and poles as I tried to paint. They were very good and even though I was within ten feet of one pole being removed, they seemed unfazed and did not ask me to move. It was uplifted effortlessly onto a lorry within minutes.

By this time it had become unbearably windy so I was glad to reconnoitre my next possible painting scene at nearby Hemsby. It is many a year since I was here and could not believe it has Vegas amusement arcades and caravan park image. A further look next time to find something more pictorial will be necessary. Rain stopped play so I headed home.

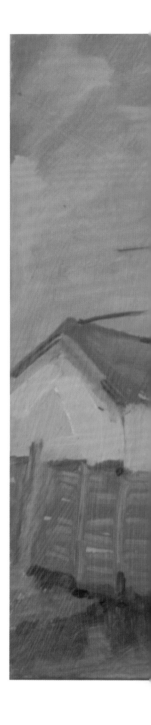

27. Scratby Marrams

Monday October 6th 2008

28. Hemsby Sand Dunes

Oil 15 x 10"

Location: On the beach car park between lines of sand dunes.

Weather: Sunny start with a few wintry clouds. Became quite dull and cold by mid-afternoon.

Comments: Arrived in good time at Hemsby at a stop that I had reconnoitred after my last visit to Scratby. It was quite peaceful as I was in the beach car park, to the left of the main one. The road was flooded on its approach but luckily was only about a foot deep with a hard bottom.

There is quite a nice valley at this spot with some attractive wooden buildings nestling amongst the marram grass covered dunes.

It seems as I progress northwards, any sunny day has the sun shining on my back. OK for comfort but I prefer painting 'contre jour' as they say. The resulting picture came out very bright and I was able to resolve it after much effort. The background noise wafting over the hill from the amusement arcades didn't help with Antony Newly urging me to "Come outside" from the sixties together with "I want to be Bobby's girl". My goodness, these songs took me back a few years but didn't help to complete the picture.

Later the same day
29. Winterton Cliff Top

Oil 20 x 12"

Comments: I took my lunch in The Dunes Café which I was surprised had a quite upmarket menu with homemade carrot and coriander soup, ciabatta with fillings and crab and prawn baguettes. Well done. I sat outside in the sun and observed the passersby at this lovely spot adjacent to the coastguards look out post. Scatby wind farm was on the horizon and the old Hermanus Hotel to my right. I once worked for the owner, a Mr Temple, at The Palace Hotel in Buxton Derbyshire. The Hermanus Hotel is noted for its thatched round hotel rooms called rondavels, an idea brought back from South Africa. Mr Temple also owned the Colne House Hotel at Cromer, I believe. A great place Winterton, and what a difference a couple of miles make from the hullabaloo of Hemsby. Winterton village remains virtually unspoilt with The Fisherman's Return pub still going strong. A place I have visited many times over the years. Fabulous beaches and dunes stretching for miles in both directions. I attempted a larger than average picture to try to record something of the drama of the coastline at this point. After a few hours of labour it was time for home. I will be away in Bath this week and hope to continue my journey with my daughter Natalie joining me on Friday weather permitting.

Friday October 10th 2008

30. Waxham Great Barn and Hall

Oil 24 x 10"

Location: Beach slip road Waxham, opposite Waxham church.

Weather: Cold start but forecaster's sun eventually broke through. A fresh breeze developed

Comments: Today was a red letter day for me as my daughter, Natalie, joined me for a 'day out painting with Dad'. After finding old painting gear for a box easel and palette she was soon well into a pretty good effort considering lack of practice since her degree course in Fine Art at Southampton Institute. After climbing the sand dunes we eventually set up painting positions on top of an old second world war concrete pill box.

It seemed like a good idea at the time but we both struggled with the increased wind blowing off the land. Natalie painted the coastline to the left looking towards Horsey whilst I focused on the Old Hall with Great Barn and Waxham church in the background. Because of the conditions my painting became pretty vigorous and I am not certain if it worked. The last time I painted the same subject on a hot summer's day it was much more detailed. That painting now hangs in Seville at my nephew Adam's and his wife Belene's house.

This coastline is very dramatic with it's high sand dune banks, much favoured by Edward Seago as it was probably one of the nearest points for him to paint the coastline from his nearby house at Ludham.

On completing our paintings we had a very nice lunch at the Great Barn's tea shop and learned a little about the largest and finest barn in Norfolk, dating back some 400 hundred years. It was in a derelict state in the 1970's having lost the remains of its' roof in a storm. Now beautifully restored,

30. Waxham Great Barn and Hall

audio aids tell of it's history with much of its' beams being salvaged from shipwrecked vessels, masts and oars making up part of its roof trusses. Corner stones are from indigenous flint taken from dissolved Priorys and Abbeys which would have been imported into the county between 400 and 500 years ago. The adjoining Waxham Manor House depicted in my painting was presumably built at the same time as the Barn was in 1580. The Barn itself was made larger to outdo those Pastons down the road. Incidentally , at the time of the Spanish Armarda local militia men kept watch on this part of the coast for passing Spanish ships whilst cannons at Sea Palling and Horsey stood by to repel enemy ships. A wild and dangerous part of the coast then as it is now, with sea defences being breached in the 1953 floods with much loss of life.

After a brilliant time at Waxham, Natalie and I made our way homeward calling in to see my sister Anne and her daughter Annabel and partner Lee for a well earned cup of tea.

Monday 13th October 2008

31. The Dunes, Waxham

Oil 18 x 12"

Location: On the dunes about 500 yards from the main beach pathway, facing northwards.

Weather: Quite dull all day contrary to forecast of sunny intervals. A light breeze.

Comments: For once I decided to make a bit of an effort to find the perfect spot and walked quite a long way along the top of the marram grass which was no mean feat with my easel and sundry equipment.

I was spurred on by Seago's painting of the dunes here and had to walk some distance as scrub and alder had grown up since his days, which were disrupting the view. It was well worth the effort with uninterrupted views of sand and sea to my right and Sea Palling and farm land to my left.

In recent years they have added some off shore break waters which have dramatically altered the line of the beach. It was quite bright to start with, the light coming from over my left shoulder. This gradually faded. A pity really as I could see Happisburgh lighthouse in the distance and possibly a tall land built mast, perhaps Bacton gas terminal.

The painting proceeded quite well with its' muted colours and I was able to start back to my car by lunch time. What struck me about my visit there was the different cacophony of distant sounds. Crows in a rookery nearby making a fearful racket, seagulls wheeling and calling to me whilst overhead I could hear the constant drone of helicopters serving the rigs off shore.

I didn't speak to anyone all this time but the sounds of the off shore breakwaters helped to brighten my day.

32. Beach Road, Sea Palling

Oil on board 10.5" x 10.5"

Location: On the road facing the beach ramp sandwiched between cafes and pubs.

Weather: Afternoon light quite dull.

Comments: After the peace and quiet of Waxham, Sea Palling was its' usual busy self. After parking, I went across to Sandy Hills Family Amusements for a bite to eat served by the charming Deborah Roberts. The café itself was badly hit by the coastal flood in the fifties and has an interesting collection of photos and newspaper cuttings of this terrible time. Many heros and much sadness by the time night was over and the full destructive power of the sea could be witnessed.

I stood my easel in front of a little row of cottages built in the traditional style, and I must say they were a pleasure to the eye. One in particular was half timbered and the owners came out to talk to me disappointed that I was not painting their home.

The large ramp that leads up to the beach took my eye as it gave me the opportunity to depict figures appearing and disappearing on its' slope. It was topped with a large blue beach flag to add a little artistic touch to the scene. It was getting cold by now in the late afternoon and I was thankful the picture was comparatively small. Homeward bound via Stalham and was delighted to hear and witness two long lines of geese in V formation heading northwards, calling to each other as they went.

70

32. Beach Road, Sea Palling

Tuesday 14th October 2008

33. Cart Gap Boats, Eccles

Oil on board 16" x 8"

Location: The car park adjacent Happisburgh's new lifeboat station.

Weather: Cold and dull day threatening rain later.

Comments: I approached my destination via the Yarmouth road and Potter Heigham direction. Although longer, it seemed much quicker missing out all that cross city traffic. Finding a good place to paint was another matter with row upon row of endless seaside wooden beach/seaside houses. I did stop at one point but a horsey lady told me I could not park there which was a bit unreasonable I thought, as this time of the year there is no holiday traffic clogging up the unmade up roads.

At the end of Eccles I found a good car park with some nice boating subjects to take my attention. I spoke to various ladies walking their dogs. One woman had some King Charles spaniels who parked in front of my easel and asked if she was blocking my view. She was. A nice fellow artist from Suffolk stopped and set up his easel 100 yards away facing inland. He gave me the space I needed rather than crowding me. Artists do not have exclusive rights over their environment but need to work quietly as painting takes a great deal of concentration.

Later that day, Tuesday 14th October 2008

34. Happisburgh from Dungannon Lane

Oil on board 16" x 8"

Comments: Although the weather was very dull by now, a distant view of Happisburgh brought back many memories. My family owned a beach chalet on Cart Gap which went over the cliffs in the '53 floods. Lovely family holidays on the beach and traipsing unsupervised in the open countryside, unlike today's youngsters. In the evening we spent a great deal of time outside the Happisburgh Hill House pub whilst my parents and friends enjoyed themselves. One such evening my Uncle Peter got into a light ale drinking competition, winning it, but on returning home on his bike, came off downhill and fell into the hedge and ditch. Happy Days.

The pub, though you would not think it, had a literary connection with Sir Arthur Conan Doyle who stayed there whilst writing 'The Dancing Man'. More recent visitors included Henry Moore, the sculptor and Barbara Hepworth , though they were sadly not to settle in Norfolk but set up their artistic colonies in Cornwall.

Before calling at the pub, I tried to get tea at the Tea Rooms at the cliff edge, now sadly closed because of cliff erosion. Let's hope the rocks that they are being deposited on the beach will stem the rot and save what could ultimately be the village. One cannot imagine Happisbugh without a lighthouse or church.

34. Happisburgh from Dungannon Lane

35. Happisburgh Lighthouse

Oil on board 15" x 12"

Location: The outskirts of Happisburgh from the Ruston side of the village.

Weather: A bright sunny day with a keen breeze coming from the southwest. Bracing but not too cold yet.

Comments: I had a bit of a rush on today with a dental appointment after lunch so I was glad to attempt a simplistic subject, for me.

My car and easel were parked at the entrance to some buildings but the owner soon came out and asked me to move to one side. This was Ok but slightly altered my angle of vision. These things are part and parcel of an artist's life. I always find this a cracking subject having previously sold a similar view to James Brett, antique dealer of Norwich. Although I have never been inside the lighthouse I could not help myself from smiling with the thoughts of Anneka Rice and her happy band of helpers working to paint the lighthouse itself in 'Challenge Annika' in a few short days. My niece Caroline Gale has stayed a few times in one of the adjoining lighthouse cottages for family holidays, and to be near her mother Anne, my sister.

It was great fun to paint an upright picture for a change and I look forward to seeing it come to light a bit more with a splendid frame.

Patrick Barwill

36. Ostend

Oil on board 16" x 11"

Location: The cliff tops at the end of a road called Ostend Place, a cul de sac.

Weather: Another fine day with hardly a cloud in the sky. Quite chilly but luckily no strong breeze.

Comments: As I painted at the top of a concrete gangway to the beach there was a constant passage of dog walking locals on their way to the beach for exercise. I asked one man about the exact location of where I am as villages along the coast have a tendency to merge into one another. We talked about the weather and strong storms here in the winter that uncovered bricks and parts of buildings which were thrown up onto the beach. One year he found the radiator cover from an old Austin 7. It was gone with the next tide. It really is a lovely view here as I faced back towards the Happisbugh direction. Ostend is a sea of cliff top dwellings in all forms of wood and brick construction. Lets hope the wooden sea defences here hold fast.

Feeling quite tired today, I expect, suffering from the trauma of the dentists yesterday. So I finished my painting and made my way along the coast to artist friend, Paul Darley, attacking his second picture of the day of Cromer fishermen.

I eventually called in at The Saracen's Head at Wolterton to check on my pictures displayed there. Robert and Daphne were in good form after a spectacular Trafalgar dinner the night before. I saw Rachel's new puppy, Hero. A real sweetie aptly named after Horatio, I should imagine.

36. Ostend

Friday 24th October 2008

37. Walcot

Oil on board 16" x 11"

Location: Adjacent the Walcot gap on top of the sea wall

Weather: A cold and drizzly start, brightening up by mid-morning with sunny skies.

Comments: On the previous visit to Ostend I had to look for a promising spot to paint so wasted no time with my subject. I precariously placed my easel on top of the sea wall which left only a few inches either side between me and disaster. Quite a lot of cars with dog walkers passed by with nice comments. A kind lady took my photo and said she was spurred on to do some painting after seeing me. I spoke at length with Mrs P Howard and a Mr P Jarvis who expressed an interest in the picture as they lived close by. One man asked me a bizarre question "Did I use the feathers from a woodcock for any of my brushes?" "Just the pig "I replied, "well Hog actually".

The coastline at this point is quite dramatic with its gentle curve of concrete sea wall linked with wooden groynes stretching out into the sea. I well remember visiting Paul Martin's parents who lived close by and whose property was regularly cut off by the sea, though not damaged like so many others along this section of coast road.

This particular subject has been painted several times by Ian Houston who manages to capture the drama of the coast at this point. He used to teach at North Walsham High School for Girls where my wife Christine attended. He was her form teacher one year, although he did not teach art, but was a music teacher there. I once went to a painting demonstration in The Ivory House in Norwich where he discussed painting with musical references. Quite interesting.

By lunchtime the sun had broken through and I was ready for a coffee and decamped to the Kingfisher Café on the front, very clean and smart. I noted a reproduction print on their wall by Harold Harvey that I hadn't seen before. Homeward bound this time via Edingthorpe and North Walsham for a change.

37. Walcot

Monday October 27th 2008

38. Bacton

Oil on board 18" x 12"

Location: The coastal path at the end of Beach Road and adjacent to a gap in the sea defences for coastal rescue vehicles..

Weather: A bright day with clear skies but quite cold, with a light breeze coming from the west.

Comments: As I made my way to Bacton I decided to take the quiet lanes from North Walsham which really were a delight going through the autumnal woods near Edingthorpe, past pretty cottages and houses seemingly untouched by time. The road eventually reappeared at Bacton fish shop, a place I used to visit on many a Saturday night after the pub. It was much favoured by my friends Jimmy and Sue Key who farmed at Honing, down the road.

When I started work, one would think the Bacton Gas site would not necessarily be an interesting subject to paint but it added drama to the picture with the coastline stretching in to the distance towards Mundesley-on Sea. One or two dog walkers stopped to chat and a few brave children played on the beach as it was half-term. I was offered, but declined, a cup of tea by a nice young lady. A caravan owner nearby, Peter Costin, from Essex, expressed an interest in the picture so I told his daughter I would forward an invitation to my exhibition in due course. It's amazing how the gas site blends into the landscape. I well remember standing on the beach all those years ago as the first pipe was pulled ashore into a deep channel cut into the cliff face, an incredible feat of engineering. My father-in- law Billy Pearson worked on X-raying the pipes, like so many other local people, glad to get quite highly paid work

for this area. Pubs, hotels and restaurants at that time flourished and to this day the site provides much needed employment. Bacton the village, to me, has changed little since I was a boy. I noticed, sadly however, that the café and shop on the coastal road opposite the ship was boarded up and for sale. This at one time before the war was owned by my father-in- law, changing hands many times since then. Billy Bingo, as they called him, and Colin Ewan had business interests in this area with caravan sites and slot machines. I came into contact with them during the development of the Bacton gas terminal.

In the end the cold weather beat me and I went to reconnoitre Paston, the village for the next painting. I am unsure if this week with the poor weather coming up, I will be able to do any more painting. In addition I am proposing to update my website, have jabs for a future trip to India in November and making a London trip on Thursday.

DOCTOR'S FARM.

BAC

38. Bacton

Tuesday 11th November 2008

39. Paston Great Barn

Oil on board 12" x 8"

Location: On the coastal road adjacent to St. Margaret's Church facing The Great Barn.

Weather: Very cold and quite windy but highlighted with sunny spells.

Comments: It has been a week now since I have painted en plein air and I was glad to get going. I approached my subject, The Great Barn, with gusto. Although not quite as long as a previous painting of Waxham's Great Barn, it was magnificent none the less and beautifully restored. This barn, however, is not open to the public because it houses a rare colony of Barbastelle Bats, breeding colonies of Natterer's Bat ,Brown Long-eared Bats and Common Pipistrelle bats also inhabit the barn. Quite a lot of wildlife information can be found on the visitor's plaque outside and on finishing my painting a visit to St. Margaret's church next door proved worthwhile. It has high vaulted ceilings and houses two spectacularly mounted memorials to two of the Paston family. The Pastons, a wealthy family, made famous by the series of letters they made between family members dating back to Henry and Edward's time, providing us with important historical information of their daily lives. There is also a small memorial plaque to Arthur Mack who was killed at the battle of the Somme, poignant as I was there on the anniversary of Armistice Day.

Going back to my picture I was in two minds to paint it as I suppose part of my coastal journey should show quite an element of sand, sea and cliffs. I could not access them from this point on the landscape. I spoke to a nice couple visiting the church who said my work was coming along nicely. A good job I did not comment on his bright red jumper, quite appropriate as we head for the festive season!

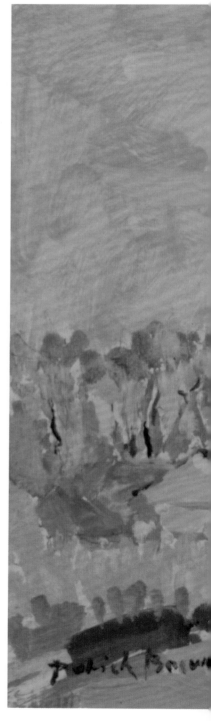

Boswells Coast

Later the same day, Tuesday 11th November 2008

40. **Stow Mill, Mundesley**

Oil on board 8.75" x 7"

Comments: This week I have to go to the Beaulieu estate on the Hamble, which is followed by Christine's mother Marjorie's birthday, can we believe it, she will be 101!

I had to make a special effort to start this painting with the cold and limited time left. The owner, who has a small gift shop, served me a coffee and said that he has been here 10 years this January. We chatted for a while until he was joined by a friend who said he was off to France on Sunday to renovate his cottage and would be gone some months. He was nursing a bit of a hangover after his farewell party the night before.

The mill itself is beautifully restored and makes a lovely subject. I really should have taken a more distant position to give it greater drama. I told the owner that my parents had lived at The Mill House, Mundesley. He told me he had old photos of when the mill itself stood there.

A quick drive through Mundesley, past the Royal Hotel which I managed for a few years for my father in the boom times for this part of the world with the influx of gas and pipeline workers which made the bar tills rattle with American cash.

40. Stow Mill, Mundesley

Wednesday 19th November 2008

41. Coal slipway, Mundesley

Oil on board 15"x 12"

Location: On the beach adjacent to the old coal yard slip road.

Weather: A rather dull start to the day but by mid morning it had brightened up. Wind was from the north west with quite a sea swell running.

Comments: Having deferred a painting trip from yesterday I was determined to venture out today. Glad I did as it was terrific on the beach with big rollers coming in. I thought I had judged the tide correctly but had to retreat three times before my painting was finished.

Mundesley seemed to have loads of dog walkers who were quite friendly, the owners, that is. A man who had a comparatively new house at the base of the slipway kindly said I could park my car there. A relief as the nearest parking was on the seafront.

I painted looking along the beach with the beach café and Manor Hotel on the cliff top in the distance. Mundesley I knew very well as Christine and I had our wedding reception at The Royal Hotel in 1973.

My parents eventually spent their retirement at The Mill House in Mundesley, father lavishing loving care on his hill top garden and making a feature of the old water wheel beside the mill pond. His charitable collecting box raised many a pound for local good causes supporting Mundesley Inshore Rescue and others.

The village though basically the same retains its old seaside charm since my time here. My mother-in-law, Marjorie Pearson, still lives here and we celebrated her 100th birthday with a party for 75 people at the Church Rooms last year where she danced the night away. It must be the Mundesley air that gives you longevity.

Pictorially Mundesley has a lot to offer the artist with its fine sea front and dramatic cliffs. The old sanatorium hospital at Mundesley at one time in the 1920s saw Mark Gertler, a prodigious artistic talent, convalescing from tuberculosis. One of my favourite artists, Peter Greenham, known for his enduring and stunning beach paintings, painted here whilst on family holidays.

COTTAGES MUNDESLEY

41. Coal slipway, Mundesley

42. Vale view road, Mundesley

Oil on board 10.5 "x 10.5"

Comments: After stopping for a quick coffee with Marjorie Pearson I decided to revisit the old slip road that runs down to the beach by the Ingleside Hotel. As time was marching on and the sun was very low in the sky I decided not to go down to the beach but painted on the cliff top not far from a bench dedicated to Catherine Lovelock and inscribed 'her favourite view' and I can see why.

To the north lies the dramatic cliffs stretching onward, dark and forboding, protected by revetments and wooden groynes. To the south stands the old Hotel Continental still proud but not quite the same glory as when I knew it as a thriving hotel. Mundesley, like so many of these seaside villages stands in a hollow of land which in times past probably made a living from longshore fishermen launching off the beach.

Coal was lighted and moved up the slipway by horse and cart from waiting ships. In the days of coach and horses they passed through Mundesley carrying goods and passengers from Kings Lynn to Yarmouth in the south. It is even rumoured that Nelson stayed at The Royal Hotel as a lad. Who knows?

42. Vale view road, Mundesley

Wednesday November 26th 2008

43. Church Road, Trimingham

Oil on board 11" x 9"

Location: By the lychgate to the church of The Head of St. John the Baptist, Trimingham.

Weather: Cold and very dull day to start with, showers mid-morning but the sun came out by midday.

Comments: I approached Trimingham via the 'quiet lanes' coming from the Southrepps direction, past the Old Rectory and a further large house not far from there where Sheila Lawrence and Suzanne Spray spent many a happy hour landscaping and creating a garden for its often travelling owners.

The position of my painting was just down the road from the gable end of the former old post office and shop, once owned by Christine's aunt Alice and where her father and his siblings all lived. One of those long since gone businesses in the country where you could buy anything from sweets to shoe laces.

My painting was stopped half way by rain so I decamped into the adjacent church, much admiring a watercolour of the church painted, I believe, by Sir Alfred Short. Amazingly, it was exhibited at one time in Buenos Aires as an example of good English art. The church, I believe, is only one of two in the country that bears the name 'The Head of St. John the Baptist, and was, in the Middle Ages a place of pilgrimage to visit to see his head., which was more than likely to be made of alabaster. Opposite the church are various cottages bearing the name 'pilgrimage' in their titles.

Trimingham itself has a little connection with my London days when I was a member of the 'Private Starlight Cinema Club' in the Mayfair Hotel in the West End. The manager, a Mr Troke came to live here and helped with picture restoration that I gave him from time to time, a fair while ago. With the sun eventually coming out I quickly finished my painting trying not to alter its originally winter tone.

43. Church Road, Trimingham

Same day, Wednesday 26th November 2008

44. Hungry Hill, Sidestrand

Oil on board 16" x 6"

Comments: This is a view that I have painted once before, bought by James Brett of Norwich many years ago. It particularly appealed to me because of the undulating landscape looking back in the Trimingham direction. The sun kept coming and going but I eventually settled on a low key painting which I was quite pleased with. Painting on the apex of the sharp bend caused a few problems with motorists but thankfully no accidents.

On finishing ,I made my way to Cromer, calling on fellow artist Paul Darley painting on the beach. The local grapevine travels quickly in this part of the world as someone had told him I was painting in Trimingham that morning.

44. Hungry Hill, Sidestrand

45. The House in the Clouds, Thorpe Ness

Oil on board 11.5" x 9"

Location: Between the golf club teeing off area and the club house, Thorpe Ness.

Weather: A bitterly cold day about 3 degrees centigrade with a biting easterly wind. A low winter's sunshine was seeping through.

Comments: It was my first visit to Thorpe Ness and driving briefly around the village getting my bearings was quite a revelation. The village created by the Stuart Ogilvie family in 1911 has its' own iconic style centred around the meare (spelt with an 'a' as the water was originally brackish). The houses give their own estate look, not quite so elaborate and ornate as the Dunwich estate houses but attractive in their own right. Spoilt for choice, painting on the beach was ruled out because of the bitterly east wind off the sea so asking at the village store for a good landmark I settled on the building called 'The House in the Clouds", an old water tower clad in wood and shaped like a house at the top. I liked the placard outside the house.

" The fairies really owned the house,
Or so the children say,
In fact they all of them moved in
Upon the self-same day."

My painting shows the golf club flag, house and a lovely Suffolk Postmill to one side, surrounded by pine trees. The club were really friendly and gave me permission to park close by, a former club captain took several photographs of me. Although the finished picture was quite colourful I fell into the compositional trap of having several items spaced equally apart. Overall, I could have stayed longer in Thorpe Ness with its' meare based on literary connections.

The family were friends of J.M.Barrie, islands were named Puck of Pook's Hill from Rudyard Kipling; Peggoty's House, Charles Dickens; and The Pirate's Lair ' from R.L.Stephenson.

45. The House in the Clouds, Thorpe Ness

The Same day
46. Sizewell Village

Oil on board 20" x 8"

Comments: I never thought that a trip to Sizewell nuclear power station would be interesting from the artistic point of view. Having spent some time with the development of Bacton gas site further down the coast I braced myself for an eyesore. In point of fact Sizewell is delightful with lovely cottages nestling hard against the shingle bank, with fishing vessels like at Dunwich, Cley and Salthouse clinging to the shore.

The power station itself sits well within the landscape and with the sunlight today on its shiny surface giving it a dramatic pose. I painted in a dip in the undulating grassland between shingle and boats and an old wooden clad fisherman's house with an unusual oriel window in the shape of a 'V' to give views up and down the coast. Quite a few people stopped and chatted despite the cold. A fisherman described the adage that 'when the wind is from the east the fish bite the least', summing up his day no doubt.

A very nice lady who I think was an art teacher described painting 100 pictures for a gallery was a stressful thing to do. I thought to myself 'I have spent over 10 years painting 60 pictures a year for an annual show so I know what she means.

Finally a gentleman kindly took my photograph and said he did mainly weddings, and in particular, for the Asian community. I thought back to my trip to India recently when I attended a wedding for 4000 guests. I have never been to anything like it before with the groom arriving on a white horse attended by elephants and camels with accompanying shrill music and exotic dancers. It was

interesting talking to him as I never thought I would be able to share my experience of an Indian wedding with anyone in little old rural Norfolk.

Time is marching on and I wanted to make a brief visit to Minsmere, the nature reserve on my way home. The light was fading fast and it was a pity because it looked spectacular in the distance from the hill behind the visitor's centre. I see in the local paper that they have introduced

46. Sizewell Village

highland cattle to the marshes which should make a strange site amongst the bird wading population. Perhaps if time permits I shall return to paint although I am trying to follow the villages along the coast so whether Minsmere is a village long since gone, I didn't see much evidence apart from a few scattered cottages.

Wednesday 31st December 2008

47. Minsmere

Oil on board 24" x 12"

Location: I carried my easel to the small hill next to the visitor's centre overlooking the bird scrapes, shingle banks with the sea beyond.

Weather: The wind was from the North-East with very overcast outlook. Temperatures hovering between 2 and 3 degrees Celcious.

Comments: On entering the visitor's centre I asked the staff for permission to paint. They were worried that I might frighten the birds. I didn't think that I was that ugly. However, they were quite sweet especially the lady on reception. My attire of grey trilby, Barbour and builder's boots was in sharp contrast to the bird watchers who had telescopic cameras and tripods to challenge any film maker. I must remember to wear my socks outside my boots in future to blend in.

As far as the painting was concerned I chose a slightly bigger board to paint because of the relatively simplistic nature of the scene. I could have broken it down into smaller components but was satisfied none the less with the end result. I spoke to only one member of staff during the painting who apparently climbs to the top of the hill every day so he can get a good overview of the car park and can count the likely amount of people for lunch. Put me down for a soup I am so cold.

I think the bird population must have been in hiding when they saw me coming as I saw just a few starlings I think, crossing the landscape. By the visitor's centre a lone pheasant caused some interest and numerous blue tits were at the feeders. I would like to have a non painting

day hereto catch a glimpse of a bittern in flight, bearded tits, Cetti's warbler or green wood pecker would be quite a thrill. I decamped thankfully to the restaurant for home made leek soup and coffee to warm the frozen fingertips. I would like to think that I will paint only when the sun is out but I think not.

47. Minsmere

Friday 2nd January 2009

48. Tower Lane, Sidestrand

Oil on board 20" x 8"

Location: Edge of Sidestrand before the road descends to Overstrand. Adjacent to Sidestrand Hall.

Weather: Another cold and dramatic sky day. The wind was keen and blowing on shore, probably from the North East.

Comments: I am glad that I returned to do another picture of Sidestrand because the cottages nestling in the dell of Tower Lane have always appealed to me pictorially. A great place to live with sea views and rolling countryside. I should imagine, if one could turn the clock back, this is how small communities would have been back in Victorian and earlier times. John Crome and many of the Norwich School artists I feel sure would have gladly taken to this subject as they did in neighbouring Cromer. Fishermen and farm labourers probably occupied these cottages in the past earning their living from land and sea.

Sheltering from the wind with Sidestrand Hall to my right I was glad to finish my painting. My next port of call was Overstrand village itself where I intended painting the café with its tractors and boats on the other side of the road. Unfortunately at this time wind and cold beat me and I was glad to seek shelter in the tea rooms for a well earned coffee and cake.

My return journey took me by the Saracen's Head, Wolterton just to wish Robert, Daphne and Rachael a 'Happy New Year'. My word they were busy, even after the festive season. Good for them.

48. Tower Lane, Sidestrand

Wednesday 14th January 2009

49. Clifftop Café, Overstrand

Oil 16"x11"

Location: Painted opposite the clifftop café facing a small grassed area with boats and fishermen's paraphinalia being stored.

Weather: ; I took a bit of a chance today with quite a foggy journey first thing but the coastal area was thankfully sunny for most of the day.

Comments: A handy spot this as I had café and toilets opposite and quite a colouful scene with the stored boats. The café, incidentally, was once owned by Christine's aunt and uncle, Rosie and Hayward Kidd. She had happy memories of working there one summer when at Art School.

Facing the café are three commemorated seats, one inscribed ' In memory of Barbara and Andrew Hayward'. The sun was behind me although I was bitterly cold and worked quickly and simplistically. The sea was a flat calm and contrasted with the dark headland in the distance. After a few hours I decamped to the café to thaw out. Most welcome, I don't mind saying.

OVERSTRAND

49. Clifftop Café,
Overstrand

Later the same day

50. Cromer Lighthouse

Oil on board 20" x 8"

Comments: I was told by my artist friend, Paul Darley of Cromer, that you could drive up past Cromer Country Club and come out at the top by the light house. All right in theory but I was stopped by a dropped barrier halfway up the hill. After ten minutes climbing the kind club receptionist allowed me in and I was soon on site, so to speak. With the windmill to the left standing majestically against the skyline and the valley falling away to Cromer in the distance, and the sea on the right, I would hazard a guess that this is one of the finest views on the coast purely because of the uninterrupted light which is quite special in Norfolk. Behind me and to one side was the Royal Cromer Golf Club, a magnificent links course.

This is the second time that I have painted next to a golf club and equally as nice as the one at Thorpe Ness. If the weather had been warmer it would have been better to have tackled a larger painting. As the day wore on with the sun dipping behind the hill I headed towards Cromer for a bite to eat and a quick mardle with Paul Darley who was painting in front of the lifeboat station. We must be the only two artists in Norfolk working outside continually in mid-January. Quite mad!

50. Cromer Lighthouse

Tuesday 20th January 2009

51. Cromer East Beach

Oil on board 24" x 12"

Location: On the beach a few hundred yards South of the Cromer gangway and cafes.

Weather: Another bitterly cold day with a light wind from the South West. A few sunny hours midday.

Comments: Actually, arriving on the beach was a bit like old times as I once leased a thatched hut adjacent to North Lodge Park for many summers and traded under the name of The Little Gallery, selling my work to locals and holiday makers. Not many of them about this time of year but I had arranged to meet my friend Paul to paint together on the beach. The reality is with artists a particular viewpoint took his eye and he shoved off to the water's edge leaving me in shadow close to the promenade. I spoke to virtually no one except for the occasional dog walker keeping warm with a brisk run out. I really enjoyed painting with my back towards the town and the pier and theatre stretching away to my right.

Although Cromer has lost virtually all its wooden crab boats there is still a good mix of fiberglass ones to enhance the scene. Many have moved down from the Runtons. Perhaps beach and fishing are not so good in that area now. On finishing Paul was intent on continuing his painting so I went to the end of the

pier for a well earned warm up and coffee. On returning half an hour later he was still well into it so I pressed on while the light lasted with a new picture.

51. Cromer East Beach

Later the same day

52. Cromer Gangway and Lifeboat Café

Oil on board 15" x 12"

Comments: The decision to start this work was because conditions looked good but after a further two hours I was really cold and struggling to finish. The crab boat and tractor made a nice foreground composition but I really wanted to show The Crescent houses above and just a glimpse of Cromer's magnificent church spire.

The blue house was once owned by my sister Anne and I have many happy memories of sitting in her first floor drawing room with a glass of wine or two. With the French doors open to the balcony the listless sound of the sea and especially at night time with the coloured lights of the pier, it reminded me so much of when I worked in the South of France. A quite magical place. I digress a bit but can't go without mentioning the lifeboat café in the mid foreground which was immortalized in oil and print by the late Alfred Cohen from Wighton in his very distinctive style. His house run by his widow as a gallery was made famous because Henry Moore stayed there as a young man for his holidays. He was inspired by the odd shaped flint stones he collected from the surrounding fields and beaches for his sculptures.

Thoroughly cold and, quite frankly, glad to finish I said goodbye to Paul and beat a hasty retreat to the warmth of my car heater and the long journey home. Cromer still does it for me and I could paint here continually which won't help my coastal journey very much. The next village will be one or both of the Runtons in due course. The weather is really closing in now so I am glad to take a break in London to catch up on a few gallery openings and visit The National Gallery for their mini Alfred Sisley exhibition. Back to the drawing board for me I think.

52. Cromer Gangway and Lifeboat Café

Thursday 29th January 2009

53. Cliff Study East Runton

Oil on board 16" x 12"

Location: After taking the beach road I parked on the cliff top car park and descended the gangway to a small concrete promenade.

Weather: Bright sunshine to start with but a bitterly cold day with temperatures hovering around freezing point.

Comments: My position on the beach had a commanding view towards Cromer, the distant pier and the magnificent cliffs to my right hand side. A very dramatic scene punctuated by just a few dog walkers well wrapped up. There was just one solitary crab boat on the gangway, something to do with beach launching facilities at present. Most of the local boats had moved to Cromer temporarily.

The sky was quite clear so made the line of the cliffs quite imposing. I worked rapidly because of the cold and was glad to find the café in Runton High Street still open to warm me up.

Later that day
54. Cliff Study West Runton

Oil on board 16" x 12"

little later on with the discovery of SeaHenge further up the coastline. More of this, no doubt, later.

It was a similar situation with the previous painting rapidly executed but this time I found Lucy's tearooms opposite the Village Inn for a well earned bowl of soup and coffee. The Village Inn, incidentally was once owned by friend and patron Robert and Daphne Dawson-Smith who run the successful Saracen's Head Restaurant and Hotel at Wolterton.

The Old Pavilion at West Runton was once the venue of many an embryo rock group which coupled with The Links at Cromer put Norfolk on the pop map back in the sixties and seventies. I never did go there myself but I believe things got very lively at the timeBack

Comments: West Runton cliffs are just as imposing as their more easterly cousin and have the characteristic of being black at their base. Apparently this was the deposit of an ancient river bed pre-Ice Age with glacial sand and boulders on top. Not long ago these cliffs revealed a fossilized Elephant which was quite exciting at the time putting Norfolk on the map, so to speak, overshadowed a

to Cromer on the way home to see Paul Darley and to catch up on arty news and to see the latest crab boat painting that he was finishing for exhibition at the Fairfax Gallery at Burnham Market.

55. Beeston Regis Hill

Oil on board 14" x 12"

Location: A cliff top position adjacent to the Beeston Regis caravan south looking towards the hill.

Weather: A sunny, cloudless day with virtually no wind. Becoming colder and quite bitter towards lunchtime.

Comments: I know that I wanted to paint Beeston Bump so took the turning that I thought was for Beeston Church, missed it but ended up driving through a caravan site and out the other end. The cliffs here are dramatic especially with the drama of the hill behind.

The painting went quite well as the light remained constant and spoke to only a few people until a voice from behind said " It's Patrick Boswell, isn't it?" Richard Sutcliff introduced himself to me, a guy who worked for me in the past when I had my gallery and framing business in Orford Yard, Norwich over 30 years ago. It was great seeing him and catching up on old times. He now lives in France and imports Range Rovers from America into the country. Presumably because they are already left hand drive. He bade me farewell and I sent my regards to his mother who I saw last year in Jarrolds when I was launching my book Boswell's Norwich. It's a small world.

After a few hours my work was done and I sped off to Sheringham while the light was still good.

WEYBOURNE

Later that day

56. The Promenade Gangway, Sheringham

Oil on board 14" x 12"

Location: I set up my easel at the end of the main street opposite The Two Lifeboats PH looking northwards.

Weather: It was still a fine day but the light quickly faded by lunchtime.

Comments: Because it was half term Sheringham was surprisingly busy and I chatted to a few holidaymakers who were interested in my painting. Surprise, surprise, Richard Sutcliff and his mother came past in a French registered Range Rover and called out "Hi" whilst negotiating a right hand bend at this point. Shortly after, my nephew Daniel and his wife Jane came by which amused me as I recalled they weren't far from home, living at Corpusty. Jane had just come out of hospital so it was good to see her on the mend. Daniel took photos of me with the easel as it is not always possible to find someone for this task as I am often in isolated parts.

After lunch the light really hit the deck so I decided to call it a day and dropped into The Saracen's Head at Wolterton to see Robert, Daphne and Rachael and check on my paintings hanging there.

117

Wednesday 25th February 2009

57. Weybourne Cliffs

Oil on board 12" x 6"

Location: Parked on the beach road Pay and Display car park and painted between fishing boats facing adjoining cliffs and pathway.

Weather: A keen north westerly was blowing and the predicted sunny day had not transpired.

Comments: I was fortunate enough to have a painting companion, Paul Darley with me this time and picked him up from his flat in Cromer. We caught up with old times as we hadn't painted together since Gorleston many months ago on a really sunny day. Our painting spots were really determined about finding some beach object to stand in the lee of. Two people commented that I should have been here yesterday, it was just glorious.

Sounds familiar.

Weybourne holds warm memories for me of dining at Gasche's restaurant with family and friends. At that time it was one of the few places to eat quality food in Norfolk. Mrs Gasche would glide around the dinner bar area sitting with customers without their bidding. Quite amusing really. Great times. Weybourne also had a special attraction as opposite Gasche's restaurant was an antique shop whose eccentric owner would stand outside berating passing traffic to call in. He would wear a bright red hunting jacket with silk top hat. Quite a sight. One raucous evening out at Gasche's he invited us over the road for drinks and we took a large plate of gateaux with us part of which ended up being thrown at his paintings. He was a good sport and put up with our high jinks for some jolly company.

Mine and Paul's pictures were soon finished because of the weather conditions and we headed up the road to Salthouse.

58. Coast Road, Salthouse

Oil on board 20" x 8"

Location: I parked my car adjacent to the famous crab shop Cookies.

Weather Just the same but with increased wind.

Comments: I painted in an exposed spot on the curve of the bend near the crab shop whilst Paul, who had a different agenda to me took cover in the lee of a reed bed on the other side of the road.

I have always liked this coastal road with its' rows of Norfolk cottages huddled around the bend in the road. They are very vulnerable as the beach's shingle bank has been breached several times over the years especially in the 1953 floods with much loss of life in this area. In the centre of my painting is The Dun Cow PH which always reminded me of a similar pub which A.J.Munnings painted in Cornwall with horses and figures outside.

Salthouse changes very little and I have often stopped for fish and chips along the road. It is not long ago that it lost its' post office which is quite sad. Above the village Salthouse's magnificent church dominates and is latterly known for holding major contemporary art exhibitions every year.

The church itself featured in a large work by Edward Seago though he gave it slightly more gravitas than the church seems to command. High on the hill looking down, lies the village, salt marshes with cattle in summer and the long line of the shingle beach and sea distant. A great favourite with me.

Painting over I had a quick word with Pete McKnespiey at Cookie's for coffee and a prawn sandwich. Yum Yum.

Monday 20th April 2009

59. Kelling

Oil on board 15" x 9"

Location: Opposite Kelling tea rooms and gallery.

Weather: A dull day and really quite cold.

Comments: Ostensibly I set out with high hopes. The weather forecast was sunny but as usual the coast can portray a different message. Still, I was keen as I have had a break for a month from painting, due to helping Christine with the interior design of The Master Builders Hotel at Beaulieu, Hampshire. It took up more of my time than I had envisaged but looked simply stunning at the opening night. Still, I digress.
Kelling was being painted out of sequence as I must have driven through at speed the last time, heading for Salthouse. Apologies to Kelling folk.

The Old Meeting Rooms that now is a tea and arts centre, took my attention. A lovely old Victorian building standing beside the coast road with the memorial to Kelling war dead in front. Kelling village itself stands some one mile from the actual sea and I didn't fancy trekking with all my equipment. Sometimes

a shingle bank can look like any other. Apparently Kelling was the place a fierce battle took place between Customs and Excise men and smugglers in the 19th Century. Originally there was a waterway between here and Salthouse now long since silted up. Kelling Heath and marsh are noted for its' special scientific interest and it is also a glacial plain formed some ten thousand years ago.

Fascinating stuff but I needed a drink and food. I was amply looked after in the old tea rooms which houses what can only be described as an eclectic collection of paintings and bric-a-brac.

Later that day
60. Cley
Oil on board 16" x 6"

Comments: Having continued my coastal odyssey I arrived in Cley and could not miss out a painting of Cley Mill and village. I parked my car at the Blakeney end of the village where there is access for emergency vehicles to the coastal flood bank and pathway. I have painted this subject before and it never fails to delight. Quite a lot of walkers passed by and one American lady, after admiring my painting, said jokingly that she had come to England to help our economy. I thought, synically, that if the Americans had not offered mortgages to no hopers it might not have had such a knock on effect here. I am sure she said it with the best intentions.

In the closing moments when my work was done the sun broke through the clouds. Sods law I think.

Tuesday 21st April

61. Blakeney

Oil on board 15" x 12".

Location: On the left hand side of the road below the entrance to The White Horse PH.

Weather: A brilliantly sunny day, no clouds and a light westerly breeze. Great day.

Comments: At least today was warm to make a start. The scene was low tide and was punctuated by the Juno, a two masted barge from Morston settled in the muddy channel. I think she must be there for the summer as she had a substantial gang plank close by. No sign of life but looked in immaculate condition with dark topsides and green scupper topsides. I don't know her history but with pivotal sea legs she is well suited to our waters.

A fair smattering of tourists stopped to pass the time with me including a New Zealand lady who discussed rugby and the merits of the latest All Black side.

My work was soon done and I packed up and headed downhill to the delights of fresh crab sandwiches and coffee on the hard in the open air. Perfect day.

61. Blakeney

Friday 1st May 2009

62. Blakeney Point

Oil on board 11.5" x 9"

Location: Boat trip from Morston quayside to beach at Blakeney point.

Weather: A very sunny day with a light north westerly breeze.

Comments: I took a bit of a gamble on this trip as I had not pre-booked but after dropping off some paintings at the new Flint Gallery, Blakeney I was just able to make the boat at Morston. We set off in bright sunshine and instead of dropping me off on the point the boat set off to see the basking seals, a great bonus for me. Steve of Beans Boats gave a good commentary and apparently we saw Herring gulls, Brent geese, Sandwich Terns named after the Kent town, Black headed gulls, a Cormorant, Oyster catchers together with a rare gull whose name escapes me.

After disembarking at the beach I was hard pressed to paint a picture within the hour of the boat returning. None the less, I rose to the occasion. Matthew Weaver took my photograph which was nice of him. 11.30am saw me making the return trip with a happy band of tourists visiting one of the delights of North Norfolk. It was a beautiful trip with little sailing boats scudding backwards and forwards in the pit area punctuated by the occasional seal popping his head up to say hello.

62. Blakeney Point

Later that day
63. Morston Creek
Oil on board 20" x 8"

Location: Two hundred yards upstream from the information area and café at Morston Quayside.

Weather: The weather stayed constant with my previous painting but now a few clouds turned the setting to shadow from time to time.

Comments: I had chosen an elongated panel for my picture as it suited facing Blakeney and the church in the middle distance and allowed space to show the visitor centre on the right. A fellow artist worked steadily away in water colour a few yards along the quay. We didn't speak but exchanged a knowing nod in moments of contemplation. There were few passers by at this time but a nice man from Northampton said "Hi". He had passed a lovely week in North Norfolk with only one day of rain. That was about it really, a smashing end to a lovely day well passed. A day of seals, Sandwich Terns and Mussell lays. The next time I will return just to drink in the scene.

MORSTON

64. Stiffkey Red Lion

Oil on board 11.5" x 9"

Location: One hundred yards the Wells side of The Red Lion Stiffkey on the coast road.

Weather: Very overcast and still the remains of a keen wind left over from the last few days' gales.

Comments: My coastal journey had endeavoured, for the most part, to get as close to the sea as possible but the weather and wind today meant I had to abandon a proposed vantage point by Stiffkey's camp site.

The sky line was overcast and obscure. However, having said that, parking with permission from The Red Lion in their car park, I painted a typically North Norfolk pub with the exterior and interior being a delight. My roadside position was a bit precarious as if any of you know the village, how narrow and twisting it is. No need for yellow lines here, there's just not room to stop.

The owner of The Red Lion kindly offered to move his very smart Range Rover if it was obstructing my view. I declined thanking him. After finishing my painting I entered his pub for the first time which was a delight. Old settles and quirky décor was most attractive.

A party of apparently Dutch visitors alighted from a minibus. They were something to do with the off-shore wind farms so the barman said.

I didn't stop long as I hoped to start another painting at Wells but was really beaten by tiredness and the dull weather. I settled for fish and chips on the front and a recce for my next days painting before departure.

Monday 18th May 2009

65. Wells Quayside

Oil on board 10" x8"

Location: A distant view of Wells Quay painted on Freeman Street opposite the Wells Tandoori and the boat chandlers.

Weather: Glorious sunny day with floating cloud base.

Comments: I thought it prudent to paint Wells Quay at low tide with the old Albatross moored up. Apparently she's moving further up the quay so may not be such a familiar site in her normal mooring. Wells was awash with dog walkers as I stuck to my task without interruption. I made the seafood bar and the Albatross my focal points. The picture was quickly undertaken and as I had little time to spare on the car park I had to leave Wells and head again westwards to my next port of call, Holkham.

65. Wells Quayside

Later that Day

66. Holkham Bay

Oil on board 20" x 8"

Location: After paying the Holkham Bay gate keeper I drove down to the end of Queen Anne's drive and parked close to the barriers before the board walk.

Weather: More of the same but mustn't speak too soon.

Comments: For once I knew precisely where to paint and after negotiating the long walk through the pines with my equipment I took position on the seated area facing the bay. What a fabulous site which doesn't fail to excite me as a painter. A light breeze was continually rolling the clouds along casting ever changing shadows on the sand. Few stopped to talk but one man, who I thought at first was a warden, talked about Holkham Bay past and present. He reflected that about thirty years ago that there was no sand dunes at the entrance to the bay and that nowadays high tides only rarely come up to the rear dunes. Perhaps he is right though it certainly floods at times when I have been there.

Luckily it was low tide and there were plenty of people traffic to keep my attention. Even a group of three horses cantered across the foreground but too late for my composition. By late lunchtime I had finished just as heavy clouds floated overhead. I popped in on Tom Mead at The Adnams Wine Shop at Holkham and discussed some of the wines for my daughter Natalie's forthcoming wedding. Tom, by the way, is the brother of James, her fiancée. There is nothing like keeping drink in the family.

Homeward bound via Burnham Market to look in on Nick Greer now running Ringstead Gallery and still stocking a few Boswell originals. Across the road to purchase brown shrimps from Gurney's fish shop to complete the day.

66. Holkham Bay

Wednesday 20th May 2009

67. Burnham Overy Staithe

Oil on board 20" x 6"

Location: The foreshore at Burnham beside the car park and dinghy launching area.

Weather: Yet again a beautiful sunny day with just a light southwesterly breeze.

Comments: To sum up, a trip to the Staithe never fails to excite and I set to my task with enthusiasm. There was no activity on the water being low tide and I was interrupted by no one apart from a lady who wondered how many times this scene had been painted. The focal point of my painting was the old granary building which is quite complicated to get right with its' complicated roof structure and adjoining building with hipped roof.

By lunchtime I had pretty well finished and unsurprisingly clouds came in and things became quite overcast so I packed up and headed further along the coast for a bite to eat at the Deepdale Café at Burnham Deepdale. It was pretty full for this time of year but I must say the menu of local produce combined with low prices for fresh ingredients was impressive. I had broccoli and gorgonzola soup and freshly baked brown bread. I am saving the treacle tart for next time.

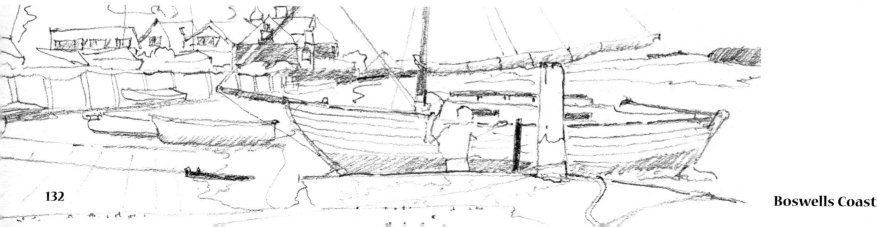

Later that day

68. Burnham Norton Cottages

Oil on board 20″ x 6″

Location: Parked on the first slip road to Burnham Norton. A line of cottages took my eye.

Weather: The dark clouds had cleared revealing more sunny weather.

Comments: The cottages at Norton that took my attention reminded me of some Arnesby Brown subjects with the washing blowing in the wind and the serried ranks of vegetables in the foreground.

The scene is set off with an old boy mardling with his neighbour. Trousers held up by braces and an old plonk hat for shade. He didn't stop long in view but I put a figure in the lane to signify him none the less.

It had been a pretty long day by now and I was clocking up over 90 miles per trip to the coast. Driving and intensely painting were taking its' toll. A day off tomorrow I think to recharge the batteries.

Friday 29th May 2009

69. Burnham Deepdale

Oil on board 10" x 8"

Location: The Deepdale Backpackers and Camping site.

Weather: Warm and sunny with a light easterly breeze

Comments: Sometimes the location just shouts what you should paint and Deepdale is no exception. As far as I know the closest to the sea is a never ending area of coastal marsh but the hostel at Deepdale is dominated by the authentic Sioux native American tipis. I suppose it is a childhood thing that attracted me to the subject as I had a book illustrating all the Indian clothing and artefacts as a child. They don't disappoint as the campsite has mounted them on slightly raised platforms to give them more gravitas.

I put up my easel on campsite pitch no 78 , nearly the same number as my painting. Inevitably, a young man who worked there engaged me in conversation. He had just returned from the European Cup Final in Rome, Manchester United being beaten 2-0 by Barcelona. He was not a happy bunny.

My painting was finished but I dream of returning to stay in one of the tipis which come with carpeting, faux fur mattresses and a wood burning stove. Many thanks to Louise Smith, proprietress, for giving me access to the site on such a busy weekend.

69. Burnham Deepdale

Later that day.

70. Brancaster Staithe

Oil on board 9" x 7"

Location: Next to the dinghy park beside Brancaster Staithe sailing club.

Weather: Still sunny but slightly more windy as this was quite an exposed position.

Comments: Another milestone number achieved in my painting journey with my 70th painting. This time I turned my attention to the sandwich stall and National Trust building behind. This is dominated by an old red painted marker buoy with Brancaster letters on it. It was a good focal point for my painting but rather a lot of red colour for this small subject.

The wind was getting stronger and I lost my hat a couple of times which made for a quick sprint to the water's edge. Luckily the tide was at a low point which seems strange as a couple of hours earlier the water was high at Blakeney as I drove through. It was a small panel that I chose to paint on but none the less was difficult to make a good composition. I hope I pulled it off. The public will decide.

Time for home and I did well to resist the Brancaster stall holders delicious seafood baguettes.

70. Brancaster Staithe

Monday 1st June 2009

71. Brancaster Beach

Oil on board 20" x 8"

Location: I faced towards the Royal Brancaster Golf Club on the beach a few hundred yards southwards.

Weather: Another hot day, can you imagine? A firm breeze coming from the north east.

Comments: Although hot the breeze from the north east kept quite a chill in the air. I have painted this view quite a few times over the years from all angles. The approach road from beach to dunes never fails to excite as you catch glimpses of the club house from time to time as the road twists and turns. At high tides it invariably floods making for an interesting journey. There were only a few dozen on the beach making for a perfect scene. A holiday maker said "On Sunday there were over a thousand people jammed in quite close to one another". All right if I wanted to paint crowd scenes.

The links course is just the other side of the dunes. Juxtaposed with the chatter of holidaymakers you can hear the clink of driven golf balls quite close. A lovely scene which I hope I did justice to.

Later that day

72. Titchwell Village

Oil on board 10" x 8"

Location: The road off the village in the direction of White City, none the less..

Weather: More of the same

Comments: I dithered about at this point in time as my original intention was to paint at the nearby Titchwell Marsh Nature Reserves run by the RSPB. The distance I would have had to have walked to the beach from this point with my equipment was prohibitive.

I was certainly not dressed for the part as a lot of people carried the most enormous cameras and binoculars on tripods. On returning to the car park a woman stopped me by the arm and pointed. I thought she was trying to show me some rare bird. It turned out to be a robin only a few feet away. So tame.

I returned to the village itself and located St, Mary's church which is really lovely with its early round tower but alas locked this day. I was intrigued by the cottages close by as their garden walls as well as gate posts had been decorated with knapped flints. I had never seen posts in this form before, most unusual. Across from this I looked back on the little village with its' Victorian cottages in flint and carrstone. They reminded me of similar estate cottages at Dunwich earlier on in my journey. A lovely little scene soon finished so I set off for home carrying on the coast road stopping off at the Orchard Tree at Thornham. The barman was French so we had a little chat en francaise. You can tell this is north Norfolk as the notice board outside offered barbequed lobster cooked to order. I am saving up.

Tuesday 6th June 2009

73. Thornham

Oil on board 20" x 8"

Location: Adjacent the old coal building at Thornham quayside.
Weather: A beautiful sunny day with a light north easterly wind.

Comments: It was great to get out of the house as my movements are restricted at the moment with Christine's mother having had a bad fall, hospitalised and then coming home to us. At 101 it is remarkable how well she is doing.

I decided not to paint the usual old coal building which pretty well makes up the approach to Thornham marshes and concentrated on the view with the old sluice gates to the left and boats bobbing in the creek at low tide in the foreground. Not too many people about which is the beauty of this part of the world even better in the height of summer.

73. Thornham

The painting went well and I was only occasionally interrupted by cyclists and coastal walkers. I often wonder where they go to after seeing me and later on in the day painting further along the coast four of them popped up three hours later at Holme next the sea. It only took me ten minutes in my car to make the journey.

Later that day
74 .Holme-next-the-sea
Oil on board 16" x 6"

Location: On the sea wall halfway between beach road and the visitor's centre at Gorepoint.

Weather: More beautiful weather but with a slightly increased shoreline breeze.

Comments: I avoided the car park at the end of beach road beside the links golf course and headed on the road behind the dunes towards the visitors centre.

It is the first time that I have been here and the sea wall path provided a superb vantage point over the creek towards Gorepoint. This area is part of the Norfolk Naturalists Trust and is protected. This was brought home to me in the visitor's centre when the manager received a call that people were tramping through some rare plants. There was a large party of 'A' level or Uni students doing field work. It was lovely to hear them chattering away. Oh to be young again, I thought.

I think I have turned into a bit of a twitcher as I found myself buying a bird identification book in the shop. Don't tell any of my friends.

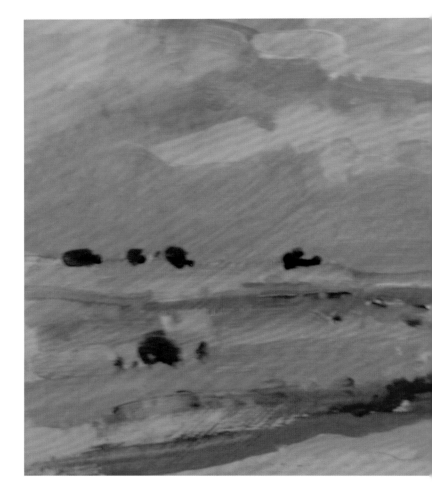

74. Holme-next-the-sea

Tuesday 23rd June 2009

75. Old Hunstanton

Oil on board 10" x 8"

Location: On the beach below the car park of the Le Strange Arms Hotel facing towards Hunstanton.

Weather: A virtually cloudless sky with a light easterly breeze following the line of the coast.

Comments: I arrived on the beach about 9.30am which was quite empty, and it stayed that way for most of the morning. Dog walkers predominated apart from a few sunbathing beach parties.

The schools haven't broken up yet so it will remain like that for the next few weeks. My painting takes in the eastern end of Hunstanton's beautiful cliffs with their layered strata. Green on top, cream in the middle and dark brown at the bottom. I suppose the brown is the carrstone seen in most of the local buildings around here.

I was mostly uninterrupted in the morning and finished a small panel quite quickly with a local commenting that I had captured the shape and fell of the cliffs quite well. I was really pleased.

Later that day.

76. Hunstanton

Oil on board 10" x 8"

Comments: I turned my attention to Hunstanton itself, a very clean, busy seaside town in the typically English tradition. Lots of promenade stalls and fun fair but with its' own 'Sunny Hunny' feel. I wasn't disappointed with where I set up my easel on the promenade because it wasn't long before the donkeys arrived near me to give children their first taste of the seaside. A subject I have painted frequently before.

In the middle distance I watched as the old second world war D.U.C.K took passengers for a ride at low tide. Great fun.

The people were very friendly and I spoke to many a holidaymaker enjoying themselves in the sun. The beach itself was surprisingly empty as the tide receded and the sand stayed wet for some time. A lovely town, a bit 'kiss me quick' but still retaining that elegant Victorian feel envisaged by the Le Strange family all those years ago. A quick cheeseburger and it was time for home.

145

Saturday 15th August 2009

77. Norfolk Lavender, Heacham

Oil on board 15" x 10"

Location: I stood on the little slip road facing Norfolk Lavender with Caley Mill and lavender fields to one side.

Weather: A truly beautiful sunny day but with strong coastal winds driving me inland.

Comments: I parked my car in the lavender farm car park and asked in the tea rooms for permission to paint on their premises. I think it was the manageress I spoke to who was very helpful and even offered me their function room for an exhibition in the winter time. Worth considering.

As usual I was a little too close to my subject but managed to pull it together in the end. The lavender was fully in bloom if that is the right word. The colour is incredibly difficult to realize. I think that is the beauty of it.

An old harvesting machine featured in my picture in the middle distance. The farm is much expanded since my youth. It now features a lovely woodland walk with beautiful plants and some rare animal breeds for added interest.

I did physically get to Heacham north beach but was nearly blown away by the wind. It's the first time that I have seen this beach and it is not bad. Inland was a sea of caravans and assorted catering facilities.

Monday 7th September 2009

78. Snettisham Beach

Oil on board 16" x 6"

Location: The beach car park

Weather: A warm day with a light westerly wind blowing, clouds building up

Comments: It was good to be back on the road again painting after my daughter Natalie's wedding at Wymondham Abbey and a quick holiday to Tuscany to recover. I had not been to Snettisham beach before and was not disappointed despite approaching through acres of caravan parks. It was high tide and the beach stretched for miles in both directions. There is a nearby nature reserve which was pretty evident, as the tide started to recede and brought in flocks of feeding birds, turning and swooping down on the mud flats.

I was painting slightly 'contre jour' but focused on a beach building built right on the shingle bank. One high tide and it looked as if it would be swept away. This is a delightful spot with very few people at this time of year. I spoke to only one man who was camping at nearby Sandringham.

Later that day

79. Dersingham

Oil on board 15" x 10"

Comments: As Snettisham was the last beach as I headed for Kings Lynn, I had to make the decision which coastal village to paint with a close proximity to the sea. Dersingham is quite a spread out village with lots of bends and is not an ideal place to stop with a car. I asked the landlord of The Feathers if I could use his car park, cheekily to paint the neighbouring pub, The Coach and Horses. I did at least, have a drink on his premises after my work was finished. The carstone buildings in this part of the world are quite challenging to paint but used The Coach and Horses as the focal point of my painting in the middle distance. Quite a few lady joggers and Mums with push chairs came by, I expect, from the nearby community centre. My work was soon done and for the first time, I headed homewards via the A47, a good indicator that I was reaching the end of my painting journey.

For my next visit I shall have to choose between Wolferton or Sandringham House itself. Probably the former as it's nearer the sea and on the A149 to Kings Lynn.

79. Dersingham

Wednesday 9th September

80. The Royal Station, Wolferton

Oil on board 14" x 11"

Location: By the level crossing near Wolferton Station.

Weather: A slightly colder day today with a light wind coming from the north, otherwise a brightish outlook.

Comments: My first intention was to paint in Sandringham Park but I could not gain access so early so I headed for Wolterton Station instead. A kind man by the level crossing told me it was owned by a man called Richard who owns the Royal Station now and who has spent considerable sums on renovation. The building just sparkles. The station used by Royal parties in the past, no longer run trains by the Great Eastern railway. It was used up until 1967 and closed in 1969. The place is quite charming with the gap in between platforms now laid out formally with box hedging. My local man who was formerly a local butcher said how the Queen Mum kept cattle and fine horses in this part of the estate. The buildings are not open to the public now but I was given access to the signal box landing stage and took several photographs just for the record.

Later that day

81, Sandringham House

Oil on board 18" x 11"

The painting went well apart from the light changing rapidly. One man said an artist friend of his wouldn't attempt a painting of three hours or more. I thought "as long as that?"

On finishing I made my way to the house which was a delight apart from the fact that the Edward Seago portraits of the Queen and Prince Philip had been relocated to their private quarters and replaced with Gunn R.A. and one other. The last time I was there was for a charity event and travelled home in a chauffeur driven car. It was loaned by a friend, Francesca, whose daughter was at school with my youngest daughter, Sophie.

Comments: I arrived at Sandringham by lunchtime and soon made my way past the visitor's centre and crossed the park to a point where I had a slight angled view of the great house. I was left fairly uninterrupted apart from a nice lady and her husband by the name of Erskine who reminded me that we had some connection with Town Close School of Norwich. She said how much she liked my Norwich book with its' connections with people that I met on my painting journey, and she was looking forward to my new book.

Homeward bound by four pm, very tired but was helped to the car park by a road train from the house.

Monday 14th September 2009

82. Castle Rising

Oil on board 14" x 8"

Location: Adjacent to Castle Rising shop and information centre.

Weather: A brisk, windy day with intermittent showers and sunny periods.

Comments: The first view for me of the Castle was just brilliant, silhouetted against the skyline, topped by the Royal Standard., the banner of D'Albini, the pennon of Montalt proudly floating on the battlements.

The massive castle was built in the 12th Century with it's earthworks and Keep. The castle itself was passed to the Howard family in 1544. Although having no roof it's well worth the time to climb its' ancient stone stairs to look at the view and also experience some of the rooms that are still very much intact.

The manager of the castle, Norman Fahy, was interested in my painting voyage and said "I might wish to link to Norfolk Heritage Explorer to find a connection with Dunwich, a village I had painted earlier on my journey. A few Americans spoke to me and a lovely man with a dog who was camping at Sandringham, took my picture and stopped to chat.

After painting I retired to the unique tearooms. It didn't feel particularly unique to me but the staff and food were pleasant enough. Home James and don't spare the horses.

Wednesday 16th September 2009

83. The South Gate, Kings Lynn

Oil on board 11.5" x 9"

Location: Painted opposite the south gate on the Lynn side.

Weather:A dry day but with a blustery north east wind offering some sunny periods.

Comments: The 15th Century south gate is perhaps the first historical hint that people experience as you enter the heart of Kings Lynn. Traffic passes through its grand opening and can be visited by the public. It is the last major piece of Lynn's fortifications. The lady in the pine shop next to me asked if I was doing it for a hobby and how much did I charge. This was a recurring conversation I had with people throughout the day and is perhaps indicative of the Lynn people's entrepreneurial spirit. Although the traffic at this point is horrendous the gateway is flanked on both sides by delightful Georgian terraced houses, some receiving a new facelift.

Painting went well until a large box van pulled up next to me obscuring my view, but I soldiered on none the less. I really enjoyed painting the subject as the gateway with its castellated turrets and ramparts is the archetypal image of a young boys' idea of a toy fort. Job done and I was on to my last picture for my diary entry, the Customs House.

83. The South Gate, Kings Lynn

Later that day

84. The Customs House, Kings Lynn

Oil on board 12" x 10"

Comments: Sadly, my journey was reaching its' conclusion. Eighty four paintings and numerous drawings later I could not have finished on a finer note. The Customs House is an elegant, classical building built in 1683. It stands adjacent The Purfleet, linking to the Great Ouse and it is so nice to see a building of such grace standing alone and not having to fight with it's neighbours for attention.

All and sundry came to talk to me and it was a bit like the time when I spent a year painting on the streets of Norwich. "When did you start?" "Is it finished yet?" " How much will you sell it for ?" and so on. Most of the people who stopped to chat seemed to be going in and out of a community centre although on closer inspection I found out this was the local probation office. Nice people, none the less.

My work was at last finished and as a passing gesture to Lynn I called into the local press office to let them know of my minor achievement. Whether they will write anything about it remains to be seen. I just felt that I had to put a full stop to my journey in some positive way.

Homeward bound but hopefully not the last trip to Kings Lynn, a city with a remarkable past and an enviable medieval heritage of buildings and churches to be discovered. Whenever I think of Lynn I think of the pictures of Walter Dexter and Arthur E. Davies, who were able to capture the spirit of the place and it's grandure.

PS Many apologies to the people of Wootton near Lynn. You were on the map but I spent some considerable time trying to locate you for a painting but gave up in the end. Very sorry.

PPS Apparently there is a place called North Runcton, also missed. Michael Caine was evacuated there for six years during the war. Not a lot of people know that.